COLE YOUNGER

Last of the Great Outlaws

BY

HOMER CROY

INTRODUCTION TO THE BISON BOOKS EDITION BY
Richard E. Meyer

UNIVERSITY OF NEBRASKA PRESS
LINCOLN

Copyright © Homer Croy, 1956. Copyright renewed © Carol Croy, 1984.
Published by arrangement with Dutton Plume, a division of Penguin
Putnam, Inc.
Introduction © 1999 by the University of Nebraska Press
All rights reserved
Manufactured in the United States of America

♾

First Bison Books printing: 1999
Most recent printing indicated by the last digit below:
10   9   8   7   6   5   4   3   2   1

Library of Congress Cataloging-in-Publication Data
Croy, Homer, 1883–1965.
Cole Younger: Last of the great outlaws / by Homer Croy.
p.   cm.
Originally published: New York: Duell, Sloan, and Pearce, 1956.
ISBN 0-8032-6400-3 (pa: alk. paper)
1. Younger, Cole, 1844–1916.   2. Outlaws—West (U.S.) Biography.
3. West (U.S.)—History—1860–1890.   4. West (U.S.) Biography.
I. Title.
F594.Y76C7   1999
978'.02'092—dc21
[B]
99-16421   CIP

Introduction

Richard E. Meyer

In an era noted for the sumptuousness of its monuments, Cole Younger's gravestone in the family's plot near Lee's Summit, Missouri, is remarkable for neither its style nor the sentiments of its inscription. There is one remarkable feature about this particular stone, however, and that is the dates carved upon it. Whatever else he may have been, Thomas Coleman Younger (1844–1916) was a survivor, and in this regard alone he differs significantly from the great majority of outlaw figures in nineteenth- and twentieth-century American history. From his baptism by violence as one of William C. Quantrill's raiders on that "dark and bloody ground" of the Civil War–era border states; through the years when he and his brothers, Jim and Bob, teamed with Frank and Jesse James to form perhaps the most fearsome—and certainly the most remembered—of all American outlaw gangs; to the blood-soaked and abortive 1876 bank robbery attempt in Northfield, Minnesota, which effectively destroyed the gang, Cole Younger stared into the eyes of death many times, and it was always death who blinked first. When he died in his bed at age seventy-two, weakened by heart disease and assorted other ailments of old age, he was indeed, as Homer Croy calls him, "the last of the great Civil War outlaws" (xv). His body bore the proof of his violent but charmed existence—the scars of thirty wounds, more than a third of them suffered in the Northfield fiasco alone.

There is an irony in all this, of course, a sort of bizarre tradeoff. One of the results of an outlaw's long life and peaceful death may be the loss of another sort of life (immortality may actually be the more operative word here), that was so clearly attained by figures such as Jesse James, Billy the Kid, and Pretty Boy Floyd. As the author of the present book points out (xv), Cole Younger had a career even more remarkable than that of Jesse James. One wonders, then, where are the legends, the ballads which celebrate the deeds of a mistreated and misunderstood American Robin Hood? Actually, there is one contemporaneous ballad entitled "Cole Younger" (appropriately enough—at least in the version I learned in my youth—sung to the tune of "I'm Just a Damned Old Rebel"), and even the briefest comparison of it to the several better-known pieces celebrating Jesse James is instructive. Using the first-person, "confessional" format often employed in folk ballads about condemned criminals (as, for example, "Charles Guiteau," concerning the assassin of President James A. Garfield), the song's tone is decidedly un-heroic throughout:

> I am a noted highwayman,
> Cole Younger is my name,
> My crimes and depredations
> Have brought my name to shame . . .

Crimes and depredations indeed! What a far cry from sentiments such as these:

> O Jesse was a man and a friend to the poor
> He would never see a man suffer pain . . .

This dichotomy of tone and attitude is mirrored in other elements of the oral folklore and subsequent popular culture treatments of the two outlaws. In contrast to the many sympathetic and heavily romanticized stories told of Jesse James, those surrounding Cole Younger tend to be grittier and more realistic. Instead of tales of befriending poor widows (which, incidentally, trace their antecedents back to twelfth century "gestes" of Robin Hood), we have the oft-repeated anecdote of Cole's attempt to test the penetrating power of a new rifle by seeing how many captured Jayhawkers it could kill at close range when tied back to back. A seemingly disproportionate amount of attention has been focused upon the outlaw's alleged affair with "Bandit Queen" Belle Starr, hardly the stuff of which true romance is made (as David Carradine's Cole succinctly puts it in the 1980 film, *The Long Riders*: "You're just a whore, Belle—I guess that's why I like you so much").

Jesse, Billy, Pretty Boy, Sam Bass, Butch Cassidy—all cut off in their prime, betrayed some would say, and all heroes in the great majority of American folk and popular treatments. Martyrdom, it would seem, does have its dubious benefits. Other factors besides an early and violent death undoubtedly play a role in the creation and sustaining of the Robin Hood ethos, but living to the stage where one's past exploits become silly episodes in a Wild West show bearing your own name and, even worse, where one feels compelled to morally repudiate these exploits under so trite an epithet as "crime does not pay" surely does not contribute to the matrix of heroic outlaw legendry which Americans seem to especially cherish. Near the end of this book, Homer Croy says, "If the war had not come upon him, Cole would probably have gone into politics" (213). If indeed that is a correct assessment of the man's essence, we may have the best explanation of all as to why he just wasn't the hero type.

Although far more printed accounts of the life and deeds of Jesse James exist than ever will be the case for Cole Younger, in a curious historiographic wrinkle the first real book-length attempt to recount the career of the James-Younger gang—Augustus C. Appler's *The Guerrillas of the West; or, The Life, Character, and Daring Exploits of the Younger Brothers* (1875)—puts its emphasis, both in title and actual content, upon the Younger clan and principally upon Cole. Of course the book is pure trash, as have been the majority of such pseudo-histories involving American outlaws. John N. Edwards's floridly written *Noted Guerrillas, or The Warfare of the Border* (1877) would help solidify this tradition, the only significant difference is that it shifts its majority emphasis from Cole to Jesse. Little would change in the decades to follow, and it would not be until 1949 and the publication of Homer Croy's *Jesse James Was My Neighbor* that a truly worthwhile rendering of the James-Younger saga would appear.

Croy, who was born in 1883, the year after Jesse James was murdered, was nurtured as a boy at the same northwestern Missouri cultural hearth that, a generation before, had produced the James and Younger brothers. The tales he heard in his youth there would remain with him long after his transplantation to the urban environment of New York City and embarkation upon a long and exceedingly prolific career as a journalist, novelist, and writer of popular literature in a variety of modes. Though today he is perhaps best remembered for his highly successful novel *West of the Water Tower* (1924), it was his conscious decision in the late 1940s to shift his energies from fiction and screenplays to the writing of historical biography which is of the most interest to us here. His subjects in this latter genre ranged from humorist Will Rogers to film director D.W. Griffith. At the heart of these works are his biographies of some of the most memorable characters of the Old West—frontier marshal Chris Madsen, "hanging judge" Isaac C. Parker, and Frank James. And if one bookend on this somewhat remarkable shelf of volumes is represented by *Jesse James Was My Neighbor*, the other is surely the work which appeared seven years later, *Last of the Great Outlaws: The Story of Cole Younger* (retitled for this Bison Books edition).

The characteristic elements that Croy employed in his earlier treatment of Jesse James are once again evident in this book—still the only really serious attempt to tell in depth the story of Cole Younger— appearing forty years after his death. We see once more the anecdotal tone, the heavy reliance upon reported conversations—some undoubtedly real, far more imaginary—and the not infrequent employment of a wry humor for which the author was well known. See, for example, the heading for chapter 10, "The Greatest Band of Outlaws America Has Ever Known Arrives in Minnesota to Look into Banking Conditions" or the solitary entries under certain letters in the book's index, "Quantrill (there's a lot about him; maybe too much)" or "Zebras were never found wild in Missouri." The result, once again, is a work both readable and entertaining, but also one that must be viewed with a certain amount of caution where the question of historical veracity is concerned. Nowhere, perhaps, is this more evident than in the numerous accounts of Cole's supposed on-again, off-again affairs with Belle Starr. (One of which would later cause Belle's principal biographer, Glenn Shirley, to remark with ill-disguised frustration in his *Belle Starr and Her Times* that "This story would have delighted a *Police Gazette* editor" [69].)

In all of this, however, it is important to remember that Homer Croy did not set out to write history in the manner required of Ph.D. doctoral candidates, nor would he for one moment considering apologizing for the manner in which he mixes anecdotal recollections with the documented record. Further, we must understand that, in the absence of a scholarly revisionist treatment along the lines of William A. Settle Jr.'s *Jesse James Was His Name*, Croy's life of Cole Younger remains really all that we have, and indeed all that we may ever have in the way of a full-length biography of this complex and enigmatic figure who shared with his more famous counterpart the leadership of one of history's most notorious outlaw bands. And that's not necessarily a bad thing either. To read Croy's accounts of the personalities of these men and the events surrounding them is to get a glimpse, as it were, of a truth behind the truth, of a place deep in the American consciousness where fact and legend cease to be distinguishable for the simple reason that such distinctions are no longer precisely relevant. Jesse James belongs to this world and so, in his own way, does Cole Younger. The hero and the survivor: we are fortunate indeed that a man of Homer Croy's considerable talents chose to give us both.

Contents

Illustrations

Foreword

COLE YOUNGER was the end of an era, the last of the great
Civil War outlaws. The county in Missouri where he was
born was the most bitterly fought-over county in the border
states; fighting here began before the Civil War and continued after peace had been declared.

He killed his first man at seventeen. At eighteen there was
a reward on his head, dead or alive, of $1,000. At nineteen
he was riding with Quantrill. He was getting around, for a
boy.

This, as nearly as I can come upon it, is his score:

He killed seventeen men.

He was wounded thirty times.

He died peacefully in bed with fourteen bullets in him. He
was not a man of much humor, but once he said, "I guess you
could strike lead in me almost any place you drilled."

He was born near Lee Summit, Missouri, and was buried
within five miles of the spot where he was born. But he made
quite a bit of history between the two places.

He was called "Jesse James's right hand," and that was a
reasonably accurate description; in many respects he had a
more remarkable career than Jesse James had. But he didn't
have a euphonious name, or the luck to die at the hand of an
assassin. Also it should be pointed out that Cole spent one
third of his life in prison, where nothing is supposed to happen
to a man. (Plenty did, however, to Cole.)

Cole and Jesse did not get along; in fact, they hated each
other. Once Jesse tried to kill Cole. The two stood facing

each other, gun in hand. But they had sense enough to put up their guns, for if one had fired, the other would have done likewise and there would have been a general mess. On the other hand, Cole and Frank James got along well together. But Jesse was the boss and the other two had to do as he said.

This is the first book to be written on Cole Younger—hundreds have been written on Jesse James—but this is the first on Cole. Strictly speaking, there is an exception. After Cole got out of prison, his first chore was to write his life. It's a small pamphlet, devoted, for the most part, to telling what a fine man he was. The title is *The Story of Cole Younger. By Himself*. He tells in detail about his war experiences during which he wore, as he constantly puts it, "the suit of gray." But he tells practically nothing about "riding" with Jesse James. And he dismisses Belle Starr in short order. We'll see later why he did this.

He trained under George Todd and Bloody Bill Anderson, two of the most murderous men who ever roamed the border counties. But Cole lived to preach Bloody Bill's funeral.

I have tried to give a picture of conditions in Missouri just before the Civil War, and to tell why so many outlaws sprang from this section. In fact, most of the great Civil War outlaws of America were born within thirty miles of Kansas City.

—H. C.

COLE YOUNGER

Last of the Great Outlaws

CHAPTER I

Cole Younger Is Born Near Lee's Summit, Missouri. Kills His First Man at the Age of Seventeen

THE FATHER of the "Younger boys" came from Kentucky, and, as a young man, settled down near Kansas City, Missouri. Living in the same county was a girl named Bersheba Fristoe. They met. The result was inevitable: fourteen children. The seventh was Cole Younger.

Bersheba's father had fought under General Andrew Jackson at New Orleans and so revered General Jackson that he succeeded in getting the stretch of land named Jackson County. Jackson County it is today. In the county are Kansas City, Independence, Grandview, and Lee's Summit, all important in our story.

The children's father, Henry Washington Younger, soon became important in the pioneer community. Not only that, but one of its richest men. Hasty writers have called him "Colonel" Younger, but he was not a military man and was never in a war or in a battle. Colonels were as thick as blackbirds on a barbed-wire fence; anybody so far down the line as to be called "Major" was sensitive about it. Younger was important enough to be elected three times from Jackson County to the Missouri state legislature. Later he became "county judge" of Jackson County. Many writers have assumed that he was a court judge and sometimes have called him "Judge" Younger. But "court judge" in Missouri was not a legal office. A happier choice would have been "commissioner," for the county judges looked after the laying out of roads, the building of bridges, and the voting of road bonds—affairs quite different from those of a legal light.

The house where Cole was born is four and one half miles south of Lee's Summit, Missouri, on the Kansas City by-pass of Federal Highway 71. As you go south, it is on the right side of the road and can be seen from the highway. It is near Unity Farms and within a few miles of land that, later, was owned by former President Harry S. Truman. The house has three rooms on the ground floor, with six above, an arrangement I never saw before.

The father began to accumulate land; it was not long before he had 3,500 acres, which was quite a bit more than even the well-to-do farmer had; in addition, he had two slaves. He got a contract as "mail agent" with the United States Government to transport the mail through this section of Missouri. The distance he contracted for amounted, in all, to about five hundred miles. To carry out such a contract he had to have wagons, horses, and stables. He was important enough to be summoned, from time to time, to Washington, D. C., to sign papers and to work out ways to handle the mail. One of the routes he operated was from Harrisonville, Missouri, to Kansas City, a distance of about thirty miles. He also managed the mail route to Hamilton, Missouri, later the birthplace of J. C. Penney. It is worth setting down here that in 1859 Henry Younger was elected mayor of Harrisonville.

Cole was named Thomas Coleman Younger after an uncle. The uncle had a beard, it was described to me, like Robert E. Lee's. When Cole got into trouble, this uncle moved to California—beard and all—to get away from what he called "a shocking family disgrace."

Cole was born January 15, 1844.

He had three younger brothers—Jim, Bob, and John, in that order.

Cole was three and a half years old when Jesse James was born; the distance between Cole's home and Jesse's was forty miles.

When Cole was four years old, Belle Starr was born. The distance between the two homes was one hundred and twenty-seven miles, as the distance is measured today.

The Youngers were a prosperous pioneer family and all seemed well. But not quite, for a black cloud lay over this section. Was there to be slavery? Or were all men to be free? The answer to that bitter question cost many lives—many in this county of Jackson, state of Missouri.

Cole went to school in a one-room building on Big Creek. One of his teachers was Stephen B. Elkins, later United States senator from West Virginia, and important in Cole's life when Cole needed help. Many of the boys were rough and rowdy, but this was not Cole's nature. He was well liked by his schoolmates and by his teachers.

The following firsthand account of Cole's schooldays was given me by Harry C. Hoffman, who lives at 6750 Imhoff Road, Oxford, Ohio, and who knew Cole many years—in fact, for a time lived next door to the Younger family. Mr. Hoffman said:

"In 1905 Cole came to stay overnight with me at my house at 2416 Walron Avenue, Kansas City, where I was living at the time. After supper he started his big meerschaum pipe going and seemed in the mood to talk, so I asked him about his boyhood. He said that the feeling was so deep in the county that the schoolboys did not play ordinary running games such as usually were played on school grounds, but war games. He said they formed into squads of soldiers, with sticks for guns, and charged and fought one another. The boys representing the Missourians called themselves 'South Side.' They always won. The boys representing Kansas were called 'Red Legs.' No boy wanted to be a Red Leg, so they had to draw lots. The feeling was so intense that sometimes, after school on the way home, the South Side boys would fly into a Red Leg and pound him. These were the conditions that confronted Cole as a schoolboy."

Later Cole went to what was known as The Academy in Harrisonville, Missouri—advanced education for those days. The principal was Stephen C. Reagan who became a captain in the Confederate Army. "Cole Younger was one of my best students."

Border war was coming closer and closer. Men from Kansas were riding into Missouri and shooting down Missourians. The Missourians promptly rode back and shot down Kansas men. Little by little Cole began to align himself with the Missouri side and finally he quit school to become a bushwhacker. It was the first important change that came into his life.

In spite of the fact that he had come from Kentucky, Henry Younger was a Union sympathizer. He thought the Union should be preserved and that slavery should be abolished—a ticklish position to take. From time to time he had Union men meet at his house and sometimes he had Southern men there, too, and tried to get both sides to understand each other. In this he made no progress, for the stake was far bigger than a rally between local men; in fact, life and death were at stake, his own life, too.

A band of Jayhawkers swept down on Henry Younger and stole a number of his horses, a number of his wagons, and destroyed property. The raid had nothing to do with his beliefs; the men wanted plunder and they got it. Cole, shocked that Jennison's men from Kansas would raid his father, turned his sympathy to the Southern cause.

There had come into being two groups, each at the other's throats. The men in Missouri were called "bushwhackers"; the ones in Kansas were "Jayhawkers." A bushwhacker was what the name implies. The Jayhawkers were named for an imaginary bird that was supposed to inhabit Kansas, called the jayhawk. Sometimes the Kansas men were called "Red Legs," from the red leggings they wore. But whatever they were called they were bad medicine.

The Missouri men were also called guerrillas—bad medicine, too.

These desperado bands might consist of five men or two hundred. They lived off the country. They stole and plundered in the name of the Union or the Confederacy, but made no accounting to either side. They wore any old thing as their uniform. So bold, so treacherous were they that one side sometimes wore the other's uniforms. In a word, a Union sympathizer would rig himself out in a Confederate uniform, shoot down his opponent, then resume his original dress. These guerrilla gangs had a distinct advantage: they belonged to no regularly organized army. They could fight when they felt like it, and then hang up their muskets when they got fed up with the job. It was a nice way to be a fighting man.

The leader of the Missourians was William Clarke Quantrill, who lived to be the most blood-smeared man America has ever known. He had been in Kansas where, briefly, he had taught school. But mostly he was a horse thief and an informer for anyone who would pay for questionable work. He had gathered a little group around him to "free the South," as he modestly put it. His power was growing and Missourians were going over to him.

Something happened that, at the time, didn't seem important. During the winter of 1861 Cuthbert Mockbee, who lived near Harrisonville, gave a dance in honor of his daughter. Mockbee was a Southerner and Cole and his sister were invited. While skirts were swinging, Irvin Walley, a captain of Federal troops stationed nearby, appeared on the scene. He asked one of the girls to dance, but no Southern girl was going to dance with a Northerner. Considerably miffed, Walley asked Cole's sister to dance, and she, too, turned him down.

Walley was sensitive over this open snub. He suspected Cole of giving the girls a warning glance, and, stepping up to Cole, said, "Where's Quantrill?"

"I don't know."

"You're a liar."

Immediately the dance was in turmoil, for Cole knocked Walley down. As Walley fell, he reached for his pistol and, lying on the floor, turned to finish Cole then and there. One of the men seized the pistol and succeeded in taking it away. Cole motioned to his sister and in a few minutes the two were on their horses and the horses were flying in the night.

Cole related to his father what had happened. His father told him he should "take to the brush." And this Cole did, early the next morning. That afternoon Walley with six men showed up at the Younger home near Harrisonville.

"Where is Cole?" Walley demanded.

"I don't know," said Henry Younger.

"He's a spy for Quantrill and I want him."

Walley and his men searched the premises, then sullenly rode away.

To "take to the brush" really meant that. The harassed person hid in the timber, or in a cave or a cabin, in fact, anywhere for shelter. He foraged for food; no chicken was safe;

fat hens disappeared with never a squawk. He stole corn from a crib and parched it. Sometimes he went to the spring-house where the milk, cheese, and butter were kept and helped himself. Sometimes a friend brought food and left it at a secret place. And there, in the brush, the poor fellow would stay for a week, or a month, or until it was safe for him to go back. Even when he came home he had to be alert to every sound.

Fon Pigg, the mayor (as I write) of Orrick, Ray County, Missouri, gave me a personal glimpse into those violent days:

"About 95 per cent of the families in this county, and in Jackson County, were rebels but peace-loving families. Many times I've heard my grandfather, Franklin Pigg, tell how he would wake up in the night and see somebody in front of the fireplace taking off his boots. Then, walking in his sock feet, the person would go into a room that was seldom used and go to bed. Sometimes the outside door would be silently opened and clothes put inside the house. This was a sign they needed to be mended; and this my grandmother would do, and in a few days someone would call for them. Sometimes, when my grandfather went to the stable in the morning, he would find one of his horses gone and a strange horse in its stall, usually lame, or one that had lost a shoe. As soon as the lameness was gone, my grandfather would replace the shoe. In a few days he would again go to the stable and there would be his own horse, and the other would be gone. This is the way our people helped each other.

"My grandfather lived in Missouri City, Clay County, Missouri. In 1863 Mrs. Harry Younger became my grand-father's next-door neighbor. The house was owned by Cole Younger's aunt, Mrs. T. W. Twyman. The four Younger boys lived at home, but had to be on the watch, for Union soldiers too yellow to fight ranged everywhere and no one at night was safe. These bands were cruel and bloodthirsty. It was known that one of the bands was looking for Cole. Sometimes he would be at home, sometimes he would have to disappear. One day Cole sent John and Jim Younger with a load of corn to be ground into meal, the two boys driving a team of oxen. Cole had broken the mainspring of his pistol and sent it along to have it repaired by the gunsmith in Independence while the corn was being ground.

"While the boys were waiting at the grist mill, Union soldiers came up, recognized them, and demanded to know where Cole was. The boys would not tell. One of the men swore an oath and said if they did not tell they would catch up with the boys on the way home and make them tell. The boys still refused. The guerrillas mounted their horses and rode away.

"When the boys went to get the pistol, they told the gunsmith what had happened. He knew the rough character of these Union men and told the boys the men would try to kill them. He asked the boys if they had weapons; one of them had, the other hadn't. The gunsmith then gave them the repaired pistol and ammunition and told them to take care of themselves. The boys knew what he meant.

"The boys had got only as far as Six Mile Church, east of Independence and which still stands, when there was a clatter of hoofs and down on the boys came the men who had threatened them. Again they demanded to know where Cole was, and again the boys refused to tell. The boys gave each other the glance, whipped out their pistols, and began to fire; this surprise action killed four men and wounded a fifth. The wounded man ran like a scared rabbit back to Independence. His name was Fox and a hunting song was made up about him. The main part was about a fox being shot in the tail.

The Younger boys unyoked their oxen, turned them loose, and darted into the timber.

"The afternoon after the shooting, a gang of these ruffians came to the Younger home and demanded Cole, Jim, and John—all three. Mrs. Younger told the men that she and Bob were the only ones at home. The men wouldn't believe her and searched the house. The three were in the brush. When the men were ready to go, they were so mad they set fire to the house and drove Mrs. Younger and Bob away. This was the reason why Mrs. Younger came across the Missouri River to Missouri City and to the home of Mr. and Mrs. Twyman.

"The men knew how to capture people hiding in the hollows and it was not long before the boys saw two bloodhounds nosing through the underbrush. The boys killed the dogs, and got away before the men could catch up.

"The house where Mrs. Younger lived is still standing. It's the second house east of the Methodist Church in Missouri City and may be seen today. My grandfather's house, as I mentioned, was next door. The two families were friends. Oh, yes! You might put in your story that my father caught the whooping cough from Bob Younger."

Conditions were steadily growing worse—the people in favor of slavery were pitting themselves against those who did not believe in it. Kansas was soon to be admitted as a state and as a result the New England Immigration Society rushed people from New England to Kansas to vote for its entrance as a "free" state. The Missourians marched across the boundary line, called themselves residents of the territory of Kansas, and voted in favor of slavery. It was a bad situation and Cole, inflamed by the growing tension, marched away and fought as a private in the state guard under General Sterling Price, at Carthage, Missouri, July 5,

1861. He was seventeen. This was his first battle. He fought in many more.

Quintrill had gathered forty men around him, the dreaded Quantrill's guerrillas. Cole joined them in October 1861. He didn't know it, but he was getting in with a dangerous gang.

Quantrill was the most murderous leader America has ever known; compared to him Bloody Bill Anderson was a snow-bank. Quantrill, with his men, attacked a small band of Federal troops near Independence, and there, November 10, 1861, Cole killed his first man, shooting him with a pistol. Afterward the distance was measured and was found to be seventy-one yards. The boy was getting a start.

All that winter Quantrill attacked and retreated, and Cole was with him. Cole was in three small engagements; by the time winter was over, he had killed another man. He was, as were all the men, fighting awhile, then hiding awhile. When Quantrill was hard pressed, he would disband his men and let each man take care of himself. When he needed them, he would call them together again. Thus Cole was living a kind of double life: he was both a bushwhacker and a home-loving body—a strange combination, but it was the way things were during those terrible years.

I had another firsthand glimpse into those violent days, this one from Martin E. Ismert, 51 West Fifty-third Street Terrace, Kansas City 12, Missouri:

"I heard my grandfather tell this story twice, and my recollection is that he told it the same both times. He was a truthful man, and I believe what he said. He was a vegetable farmer in Wyandotte County, Kansas, raising vegetables under glass, considered very unusual at that time. Once a week he made a trip to Fort Leavenworth where he sold his produce. At this time the Kansas Red Legs were riding high and handsome. They respected no one and engaged in as much mischief as Quantrill ever did. Grandpa said they were as bad as Bloody Bill Anderson, a statement that means something, if you know this section.

"One evening Grandpa was trying to round up his cows, down near the Missouri River, when suddenly he came upon a camp of five wild-looking men—enough to scare the wits out of anybody. One addressed him as Mike, which was his nickname. Grandfather surmised they were Red Legs from Kansas, but kept his thoughts to himself, a wise decision. The men said they would be there a few days, and ordered my grandfather not to reveal their whereabouts. He found his cows and returned home.

"Later that evening the leader of the men came to the house and said he wanted to buy some milk. My grandmother gave him a crock of milk. The next evening the man came back and my grandmother gave him more milk, also a pan of biscuits. This went on for four days.

"The men became bolder. One day they entered the house and demanded some biscuits of the Indian girl my grandfather and grandmother were raising. The Indian girl pointed to the oven and tried to make them understand that the biscuits were not done. One of the men began slapping her around and demanded that she tell them where my grandfather was. She said that he was at the barn. One of the men pulled open the oven door, snatched out a pan of biscuits, juggling them from hand to hand because they were hot.

"The men arrived at the barn where my grandfather was, and demanded his riding horse, adding that if he didn't produce the animal he would be sorry. Grandfather explained that the horse was out in the pasture and said that if they wanted it they would have to look for it themselves. The men buzzed among themselves for a moment, then ordered my grandfather to go out and get the horse and bring it without any more lip.

"Just then there was a sharp commotion—five other men arrived. The man who had been hectoring my grandfather turned and stared in astonishment.

" 'Boys,' one yelled to the others, 'it's Quantrill's men!'

"The newcomers began immediately to fire. Two of the Red Legs fell dead on the barn floor. The other Red Legs dashed away as fast as they could go, no one censuring them for that.

"The leader of the newcomers said quietly to my grandfather, 'The man was right. I am Quantrill.' The other men called him Leader.

"Quantrill told my grandfather that he did not want to embarrass him for what had happened, for, he said, the Red Legs would organize a search party and finally, sooner or later, find their way to the barn. Then Quantrill had his men hitch up their horses to my grandfather's wagon, put the two dead men in and take the bodies to the Missouri River and dump them in. Then they brought the wagon back and thoroughly scrubbed the bloodstains off the wagon floor. Quantrill then ordered his men to take the two horses of the dead men—the horses had been tied to posts at the end of the farm lane. And now, leading the two riderless horses, Quantrill and his men rode away, closing the incident. My grandfather said that Quantrill was a quiet, well-mannered man and was no more cruel during his life than any other leader would have been who was engaged in border warfare."

CHAPTER II

Cole Sleeps with Quantrill. Cole
Poses as an Apple Woman.
The Christmas Day Murder

Q UANTRILL was doing so well as a guerrilla, that in March
1862 he decided to attack Independence itself, an ambitious
idea. With sixteen picked men he marched—or rather crept
—toward Independence to have his way with the unsuspecting town. Night came and rain and Quantrill and his men
stopped at the house of a man named Tate where Quantrill
asked if he and his men might sleep in the house. Tate wasn't
very receptive to the idea, but what could anyone do when
Quantrill asked? A guard was posted outside, and, after quite
a bit of scrabbling around, the men were put to bed.

Among the men in the house was George R. Shepherd. He
was a tough bird, as we'll see later.

One bed had been left, and Quantrill chose Cole to sleep
in it with him. The other men were to sleep on the soft side
of the floor. Cole and Quantrill lay down on the bed in their
clothes. Soon the men were in the land of sweet dreams,
from which they were awakened by something that wasn't
sweet at all—rifle fire. The Federal troops had come up in
the rain, had captured the guard, and were ordering Quantrill and his men to surrender. One of the Federal men was
hammering on the door, demanding Quantrill's scalp. Quantrill did not want to give up his scalp and began to maneuver

for time. Locating from the voice where the man must be, Quantrill fired and killed him. Quantrill then called out to the Federal men and asked that Tate and his family be allowed to leave. The Federal troops agreed to this and Tate and his family went thankfully into the night.

A battle began, those inside firing out, the ones outside firing in, a typical battle of the border days.

The Federal troops managed, in spite of the rain, to set the house on fire. Quantrill and his men had to do something immediately. Cole made a dash out the back door and started running as fast as he could through what proved to be a patch of gooseberry bushes. This was fine, but he had departed so hastily that he hadn't had time to put on his boots. He finally escaped and so did the rest of Quantrill's men, and the next morning they met together, Cole walking as if on eggs. The fight had been so hot and bitter that Quantrill had to delay, for the time being, his attack on Independence.

For some reason or other, Cole was ashamed of the inglorious way he had fled and would never mention it. In his book it appears not at all but his brother-in-law, John McCorkle, tells the story in *Three Years with Quantrill.*

The crisis grew. While Henry Younger was in Washington, D. C., seeing about his mail contracts, Red Legs from Kansas came across the border and stole some of his horses and wagons. He was shocked when he got back, and went to Kansas City to protest to the state militia, which was Northern, and was promised protection. On July 20, 1862, he got into his one-horse buggy and started on his return trip to Harrisonville, a distance of thirty miles. He had gone only a short way when there was the sound of hoofs. Sweeping down on him was a band of men under command of Captain Irvin Walley who was bent on revenge and robbery. Walley knew that Henry Younger carried considerable money; now was his chance. With hardly an exchange of words Younger was shot. After he fell out of his buggy, the body was hastily searched, robbed of $500, and left lying on the ground. The horse was caught and tied to a tree. Then the men, having completed their work, galloped away.

A neighbor woman and her son came by on their way to Lee's Summit. They were Mrs. Washington Wells and her son Sam. We shall meet them again later, but his name, then, will be Charlie Pitts.

Mother and son were shocked by what they saw. While the mother remained to keep watch, the boy rushed to Kansas City to tell the Federal authorities what had happened. The militia arrived, put the body in the buggy, the horse into the shafts, and drove to Harrisonville where the body was given to the agonized widow. When the body was examined by the militia it was found that the murderers had overlooked a money belt containing $2,200. The money was handed over to the widow.

The murder of his father served to embitter Cole more than ever. A chance to become a "legitimate" soldier came in August 1862 when he was sworn in as a member of the regularly enrolled Army of the Confederacy. Not only that, he was made a first lieutenant in Captain Jarrett's company in Upton B. Hays' regiment, which was part of a brigade under General Jo Shelby. He was now eighteen and already had killed three men. He was bad medicine. And he was fearless. No one ever questioned that.

The strange and baffling character of the young warrior was beginning to assert itself—his ruthlessness in battle, his tenderness to those who had fallen. When a battle was over, he was a changed man and became kindly and considerate of everyone. All during the winter of 1862 he helped to nurse the bushwhackers who were having to hide out, and was sympathetic and helpful toward them. The men hid in caves and in huts; Cole would walk long distances to get medicine for them and would nurse the men as best he could.

Meantime, Quantrill wanted Independence more than a bear wants honey, but Lieutenant Colonel James T. Buell stood between him and the honey tree. Quantrill ordered Colonel Upton B. Hays to capture the town forthwith. Easier said than done. How many troops did the Union side have? Colonel Hays deliberated, not knowing just what to do about it. Then he decided the first thing to do was to find out how many troops Buell had. That was a bit of a problem, too. He determined to solve it by sending a spy. He asked for volunteers, but none of the men fancied the idea. Finally Cole said he would go.

The story of what happened was told to me by Charles J. Conard, 704 West Stone Street, Independence, Missouri. Mr. Conard's grandfather, Hiram James George, rode with Cole as one of Quantrill's guerrillas. After the war, Cole often came to Mr. George's home and there young Charley, as a boy of ten or twelve, listened open-mouthed to Cole's adventures. He heard the following story at least twice from Cole's own lips:

The men who served as spies usually went into enemy territory disguised as cattle buyers, farmers, or, sometimes, woodchoppers. Cole, after thinking it over, decided on something new and different—he'd go as an old apple woman. It was the custom for women to visit camps with baskets of fruits and vegetables. That's how he'd go.

He was able to get a wig with gray hair that had been used at country parties. Then he got a splint basket, an old slat bonnet, a pair of spectacles, and a woman's dress which he filled as tightly as a sausage does its skin, for Cole, at this time, weighed 170 pounds and lacked half an inch of being six feet tall. He was allotted a good horse and put on it a sidesaddle. He had a pistol in his pocket, fruits and vegetables in the basket. Hooking the basket over his arm, he gathered up the reins and eased gracefully into the sidesaddle. He was now a spy. All he had to do was to get the information—and come back.

He rode into Independence without attracting too much attention, and clopped up and down the street seeing what he could see. Now and then he would croak in a trembly falsetto, "Apples, beans, beets, tomatoes, and fresh vegetables." Now and then an apple-hungry soldier would buy an apple and hand the old woman money. "Thank you, sir," she would squeak appreciatively.

Finally it was noticed that she was covering a great deal more territory than the average vegetable woman did. Growing suspicious, a mounted picket started after her. "Wait a minute, Granny. I want to talk to you."

Granny rode on, pretending she had not heard.

"I tell you to stop!" shouted the picket.

There fell in behind the picket, to enforce his demands, a sergeant with a detail of six men, all on horseback. Things were getting warm for the vegetables.

"I order you to stop!" called the picket, and rode a little faster.

Granny likewise rode a little faster.

"Damn you, I'll teach you something! Stop!" bellowed the picket, now thoroughly exasperated.

But Granny did no such thing; instead, the old lady trotted even more briskly.

Spurring his horse, the picket came alongside and grasped Cole's bridle rein. Cole's hand dived into his pocket. He fired and the picket fell off his horse, dead.

Cole lashed his horse and down the road he flew, the

mounted detail after him. He had a good horse and got back to the Confederate lines, not an apple left in his basket.

Cole reported to Colonel Hays what he had seen. Hays added this to what he already knew and on August 11, 1862, attacked Independence, Missouri—not only attacked the town but captured it. The success of the attack was by no means all due to the information Cole had gathered, for many other factors were involved, but the facts the old apple woman had gathered helped win a victory for the South.

Things were moving fast.

Lone Jack was a little town a few miles from Kansas City. Originally the place had sprouted a lonely blackjack tree, a landmark on the open prairie, and so the place became Lone Jack. The town is still Lone Jack, famous in our section of Missouri.

The Battle of Lone Jack started at daybreak August 16, 1862, and it was kill or be killed. In a short time the Confederates were running short of ammunition. There was ammunition a mile away in a springhouse where a farmer kept his milk and butter. Cole mounted a horse and set off as fast as he could. In the springhouse he found a splint basket, filled it, hooked it on his arm, and raced back. He was the only man on horseback, a prominent target. He rode up and down the line, 150 yards from the Union soldiers, tossing out ammunition as the Federals tried to pick him off. Finally the ammunition was distributed and he turned to ride away. As he left, the Federal soldiers sent up a cheer. They knew bravery when they saw it.

The battle had many unexpected twists and turns. One happened to Major Emory Stallsworth Foster, who was in command of the Union troops. He had been born a few miles away in Warrensburg, Missouri, where he had recruited a company of volunteers to fight for the Union cause.

In the same town Francis Marion Cockrell had recruited a company of volunteers to fight for the Confederates. But there was only one place to parade, so the two companies— one Northern and one Southern—drilled on alternate days on the same ground. In a short time the two companies marched away to war and soon were fighting each other like wildcats. This is the only time such a thing happened in the War Between the States. It shows how mixed up conditions were in Missouri.

On this day, at Lone Jack, luck was against Major Foster and he was shot through the body, was captured, and taken to a house that was serving as a hospital for the Confederates. As he was lying on a cot, bleeding, a Confederate guerrilla came in and saw that he was a Union officer. The man's rage leaped up and, drawing his pistol, he uttered an oath and said he was going to kill Foster then and there.

At this moment Cole came in, grasped the situation, and told the man to calm himself. Instead, the man became more violent and prepared to fire. Cole sprang at him, seized him, and bodily rushed him out the door, telling him that if he came back he would kill him.

Cole saw that Major Foster still possessed pistols, and took them from him. Major Foster then told Cole that he had money with him and that he would entrust it to Cole. He handed Cole $700, quite a sum in those days.

"I want you to promise me that you will take it to my mother in Warrensburg," said Major Foster.

"I promise," said Cole, and put the money in his pocket. And he did take it there and gave it to his enemy's mother, which shows how things were done in those strange days of civil war.

The Confederates were victorious, but the Union troops were still there and meant to gobble up anybody they could.

After the battle Cole Younger was placed as a picket on one of the roads.

A young Confederate soldier came riding up and was stopped by Cole, who wanted to know who he was and where he was going. The young Confederate said he was Warren C. Bronaugh (pronounced Bro-naw) and was a member of Company K, 16th Missouri Infantry.

Young Bronaugh said also that he belonged to Colonel Vard Cockrell's company and that he was hungry, had been out foraging, and was returning to his company.

"Where do you think your company is?" asked Cole.

"Over there." Bronaugh pointed out the direction.

"Colonel Cockrell is in full retreat and is now on the east side of town, on the Chapel Hill Road. If you keep going where you started you will be captured by the Federals and probably killed, or at least imprisoned."

Bronaugh was shocked by the narrow escape he'd had and looked closely at the picket. He saw a handsome, stalwart, alert young man who wore a black slouch hat, dove-colored trousers, and a colored shirt. Around his waist was a belt with two pistols and, in his hands, a rifle.

Bronaugh was deeply appreciative. The two talked for nearly an hour, then Bronaugh rode on, and, after a time, safely joined his command, gratefully alive. He did not know the name or the identity of the young picket who had saved his life.

Thus three unusual things had happened to Cole at the Battle of Lone Jack:

The delivery of the ammunition.

The saving of Major Foster's life.

The saving of Bronaugh's life.

The latter two figured decisively in Cole's own life.

Cole's mother had a faithful slave living with her named Suse (pronounced Sooz, a corruption of Susan). She was like so many of the colored people during the War Between the States—faithful to the people she had worked for so many years although they were fighting to keep her a slave.

One night, shortly after the Battle of Lone Jack, Cole slipped home to Harrisonville to see his mother. He knew this was ticklish business and placed two of his brothers in the yard on guard if anyone approached. In no time at all someone did—Northern troops determined to make short work of the young man who was causing them so much trouble. Cole was trapped inside. It was an awkard situation.

The men shouted for the door to be opened, and when Suse opened it there were three or four men standing in the night.

"Where's Cole?" they demanded.

"Massa Cole he gone long time. You-all get out of here."

Making a sign to Cole, she picked up a quilt, held it before her, and dashed at the men, screaming at the top of her voice and shaking the quilt. The startled men fell back and, as they did so, Cole slipped out the door into the night and began to run. He was detected after a moment and the men began to bang away. But Cole made it—once again he was back in his protective coloring.

Cole was doing as he had done so many times before, and as both Confederates and Union men were doing in this year of madness. The Union men may seem more cruel and bloodthirsty, but this is only because I am giving Cole's side. The Confederate guerrillas were equally bloodthirsty and one side, so far as I can tell, is no more to be blamed than the other.

Two months after the men had come to his mother's house to seize Cole, they came again, in the middle of the night, in winter, with two feet of snow on the ground. When the men discovered he was not there they were infuriated and ordered his mother to set fire to her house. She had the four youngest children with her, boys and girls both, and begged to be allowed to wait until morning. The men went off to one side and held a whispered conversation. The leader came back and said they would wait—a fine bit of chivalry, his manner said. There, standing around a fire, the men waited till morning, just as they had so kindly promised.

The men allowed the family to have breakfast.

A bed was carried out of the house and placed in a farm wagon.

"Start the fire," said the leader, and this Cole's mother had to do. It was a dreadful, heartbreaking moment.

After the fire was going Cole's mother, four children, and Suse started through the snow to Harrisonville, a distance of eight miles. But they made it. They got there and, some way or other, managed to live.

Cole's mother left her house in Harrisonville and moved to Waverly, Missouri, a few miles away. The word about the money belt got out, and again the bloodthirsty crew came, this time demanding the money. Mrs. Younger said she didn't have it. Again the men went off to one side and held a whispered conversation. Then they came back and said to Suse, "You know where the money is. Tell us."

"I doan know," said Suse.

"If you don't tell us, we'll hang you."

"I doan know where it is," said the faithful woman.

The men seized her, dragged her into the yard, put a rope around her neck and over the limb of a tree. Then they pulled her up, left her hanging, and rode away. After they had gone, Mrs. Younger rushed out and cut her down. In a few moments Suse came to. What the men didn't know was that the money was concealed in Suse's skirts.

Whatever his shortcomings, Cole had at least one redeeming trait—his loyalty to a friend.

In October 1862, he was in command of a dozen men and was camped on Big Creek, four or five miles from where he was born. One of his men came flying up on horseback with the news that Steve Elkins had been captured and was being taken to Quantrill's camp to be shot as a Union spy. The man who had brought the news, John Hays, knew that Elkins had been Cole's schoolteacher.

Cole got on his horse and rode to Quantrill's camp as fast as he could clatter and there, sure enough, was Cole's teacher. Cole knew that Elkins was a Northern sympathizer, but Cole also knew that Elkins was a friend. Cole greeted Elkins briefly and gave him a look that meant, "Don't despair," hurried to Quantrill, and said, "Captain, you've got my old teacher and your men are going to shoot him."

"We shoot all spies," said Quantrill.

Cole, willing to lie for a friend, told a whopper. He said that Elkins was a Southerner from West Virginia and that his father and brother were Confederate soldiers, which they were not, and that it would be unjust to shoot a loyal sympathizer like Steve Elkins.

"My men say he's a spy."

"Well, they'll have to fight me," said Cole hotly. "I know him and they don't."

"If he's a Southerner, why isn't he in uniform?"

"Because his mother is an invalid and he has to take care of her," said Cole, thinking fast.

"Well, since you feel so deeply about it, I'll turn him over to you to handle."

When Cole came back, the men who were waiting to shoot Elkins were silently watching.

"Well, Teacher," called Cole, "I've got good news for you! I'm going to turn you loose and if anyone interferes he'll have to settle with me."

Cole and Elkins walked past the threatening men.

When the two got about half a mile from camp Cole said, "Here's the Harrisonville-Kansas City road. Take it and move fast."

Cole waited an hour to see that none of the men came up, then returned to camp where the men were still in an angry mood. Seemingly the incident was over.

As an illustration of how conditions were in this bitter and bloody state there was no hospital, after the Battle of Lone Jack, to take care of the wounded. The men could not even be moved to farmers' houses but had to be hidden away in caves and dugouts in the hills near Kansas City and Independence. Sometimes a hole would be dug back into the hillside, the entrance covered with brush and leaves, and there, like animals, the men would exist. Now and then there would be a skirmish between the two sides and more men would go into the caves. It was ugly.

Suddenly something reared itself up and struck at Cole. Quantrill and his troops killed a man named Judy in Kansas. The man had gone there from Missouri, was reckoned a Northern sympathizer, and was killed by two men in Quantrill's command. Cole had nothing to do with it and was not even in the fight, but the young man's father believed that Cole was the guilty one and got out an indictment against him. Cole didn't pay too much attention; they'd have to catch him first. And so the matter rested. Cole never dreamed how, in later years, it would smite him.

A good illustration of how the soldiers lived is shown by

where and how they camped. George Todd, who was the head of one group, was camped on what was called the Grenshaw Farm, about seven miles from Independence. Cunningham, another of Quantrill's men, was camped on the Little Blue River, not far from Kansas City. Captain Cole had his men on the Martin O. Jones farm eight miles out of Kansas City. Nearly every day one of these groups was in a skirmish —sometimes all were. It was not a pleasant winter.

Revenge had been in Cole's soul ever since his father had been killed. He had no reason to believe that some of the men would be in Kansas City, and so on Christmas Day, 1862, Cole gathered five men around him and set out to find the men he believed to be guilty. Leaving one of the men to guard the horses, Cole and four of his men went here and there among the saloons. About midnight they came to a saloon on Main Street where several men were seated at a table playing cards and drinking. One of the players recognized Cole and reached for his pistol. Cole was cat-quick and almost instantly the place was filled with the acrid smell of powder. Cole and his men rushed out, leaving the soldier who had recognized Cole dead on the floor. Cole and his men were pursued, but not caught. Cole had no way of knowing if the soldier who had recognized him had been involved in the killing of his father. In fact, he never did get to avenge his father's killing. But he did not care too much; he was killing off Northerners.

Colonel Penick, who was in command of the Union troops at Independence, said that this was a little too much— killing a man in cold blood on Christmas Day—and offered a reward of $1,000 for Cole, dead or alive, preferably the former. Cole was eighteen. He was getting famous in the business of war.

CHAPTER III

Cole Rides with Quantrill and Takes Part in the Dreadful Sacking of Lawrence, Kansas. The Story of the Earnest Printer

THE TERRIBLE border warfare continued. If you lived in Kansas you could ride across the line and kill a Missourian and no one would raise an eyebrow. And vice versa. It was a time of high jinks for the guerrillas, who robbed and killed and burned both their own people and their enemies. They didn't care, just so they got loot and revenge.

Much of this was due to three misguided Kansas fanatics: Lane, Jennison, and Montgomery. If they had never been born, the Union cause would have been better off. They were such supreme butchers that thousands of Union men in the border counties turned their backs on these Kansas commanders and joined the Confederacy. And yet the three acted through what they considered the "highest motives"; they wanted to free the Negroes; instead, they cost the lives of thousands of men, women, and children in Missouri's "Bloody Corner." Once Lane came back from a plundering expedition into Missouri with a wagon train three miles long.

Each side was spying on the other—the proslavery people in Missouri were watching the antislavery people of Kansas who, in turn, were watching the Missourians. Girls were

being used. Many of the girls were related to Southern guerrillas—sweethearts and wives—and would do anything for
them in this bitter warfare against the North. The Southern
guerrillas would rob and then give the money to the girls
who would buy ammunition. It was a bloody ring-around-a-
rosy.

The Federal officers arrested some of these girls who
espoused the Southern cause. What to do with them—that
was the problem. Some were put in the Union Hotel in
Kansas City, which was used, from time to time, to detain
women prisoners. Seventeen were taken to 1409 Grand Avenue, an old rattletrap of a building owned by George Caleb
Bingham, the Missouri painter who had once used it as a
studio. Bingham himself was the treasurer of the state of
Missouri—a strange business for an artist to get mixed up in.

The building formerly had been owned by Bingham's
second wife. Bingham and his family had gone off to Europe.
However, before going Bingham had entrusted his estate,
including this building, to the Reverend Robert S. Thomas,
who was Bingham's second wife's father and founder of
the First Baptist Church of Kansas City. While Bingham
was gone, Dr. Thomas lost his mind and made such bad in-
vestments that Bingham's money was gone and he had to
come scurrying home. The building—the source of so much
trouble—was in Bingham's name.

Originally the building had been two stories, but Bingham
had added a third, which made the rickety old relic top-
heavy. A word needs to be said on the building itself. Hogs
lived under it, which tells us a good deal about the place and
the times. On the first floor was a store kept by a Jewish
grocer. There was an outside stairway that led to the second
floor where the guerrilla girls were kept. The top floor had
been rented out to girls of easy virtue, which, if he had

known it, would, no doubt, have shocked the Reverend Thomas profoundly. The two groups did not get along well together. Sometimes soldiers would come and call up to the girls of the third floor, asking the girls to come down and take a walk with them. What a strange establishment it was: hogs in the basement, girls of easy virtue on the top floor.

At certain times of the day the good girls on the second floor were allowed to leave the building and go to the store in the town where they could buy things, with a guard marching solemnly behind them, rifle over shoulder. The bad girls on the top floor could leave any old time they wished, which certainly was an unjust arrangement if ever there was one.

Among the girls detained were two cousins of Cole Younger—Charity Kerr and Nannie Harris, cousins on his mother's side. And there were two sisters of Bloody Bill Anderson—Josephine and Mary. Anderson had a sister named Jenny, ten years old. After her two sisters had been taken to prison, she was lonely at home and—another glimpse into the times—went to prison to join her sisters.

The grocer tried to send word to Bingham that the building was unsafe, but Bingham was in Jefferson City and did not get the message.

A sergeant was sent to inspect the building; he reported it was safe and went unconcernedly on his way.

The next morning, August 13, 1863, there was a grinding and a roar and the building caved in, with the bricks, mortar, and beams on top of the girls, killing Bloody Bill Anderson's sister Josephine and one of Cole's cousins. The other leaped from the window and escaped with her life.

In no time at all an inflamed mob gathered and the word was spread that the building had been deliberately undermined. However bitter the struggle had grown, Union officers would not order the undermining of a building to kill girls.

But Cole Younger believed it, and so did Bloody Bill. There, as he stood in the edge of the angry crowd, Bloody Bill swore revenge. He had his own way of keeping a record of his revenge. He got a silken cord and placed it in a buckskin purse in his pocket. Every time, from that day on, he killed a Union sympathizer he tied a knot in his tally string. When he himself was killed there were fifty-three knots in the string of silk.

Bloody Bill's father was a horse thief and informer; when he was killed in Kansas he had the scalps of two women fastened to his horse's bridle. The Andersons were not an admirable family.

The building incident was just what Quantrill wanted. He would give Lane a taste of his own medicine; not only that, he would have his scalp, too. He began making plans. Shortly before this he'd gone to Jefferson Davis, in Richmond, and told him he ought to be made a general. Davis made him a colonel, which tasted worse than calomel, and Quantrill began to sulk in his tent. He'd show Davis what a great general he was!

Before that he had been, as noted, a teacher in Kansas, but he had given up teaching for something he was better fitted for—horse stealing. He went back and forth across the state line, stealing horses in Kansas and selling them in Missouri; on his return trip he would lift Missouri horses. In Kansas he was opposed to slavery; in Missouri he believed in it to the hilt.

Three days after the cave-in he gathered his desperadoes around him in the brush and told them that the time had come to attack Lawrence (named after Amos A. Lawrence, a wealthy man of Massachusetts) and pull it to the ground. What a sight he made there in the moonlight: a smallish man with red hair, a thin face, and blue eyes one of which had a sinister droop—a butcher setting up his meat block.

As he stood before his craftsmen, this strange, unexplainable, half-demented man spoke well and grammatically. He was going to start on a dangerous mission; if they wanted to drop out they could do so without disgrace.

"How about you, Bloody Bill?" he asked.

"Lawrence or hell," said Bloody Bill, not realizing that soon he would be in the latter.

"And you, Cole Younger? How do you feel about it?"

"I say sack the town."

He turned to "Fletch" Taylor, whom he had sent to Lawrence to spy on the town, and this Taylor had done, living in a fancy hotel and posing as a cattle buyer.

"How about you, Fletch Taylor?"

"Remember the girls," said Fletch chivalrously.

"And you, George Shepherd. What do you say?"

"It's the home of Jim Lane."

"What do you say, Hi George?"

"I say burn it to the ground."

Strong words, but the bitterness was so great that this was the way once-sane men felt.

Quantrill went up and down the line. There was not a man who did not want to wash his hands in blood.

"It's Lawrence. Kill every man and burn every house. Saddle up!"

It was not long until the men, numbering 400, were moving through the night to take part in the most disgraceful, most inexcusable raid ever perpetrated in America. Cole Younger was one of the leaders. And in the group was Frank James, who had been with Quantrill several weeks but had never gone on a big raid; this was his first chance really to splash blood. Jesse James was not there, and he and Cole had not yet met.

What a band of cutthroats they were, moving through the night. Many were boys in their teens, some were men in their fifties. Some had come to avenge the death of a relative, some had come for the sheer excitement of it, others for plunder. Before they are judged too harshly it should again be emphasized that this was a time of violent feelings and intense hates. Blood and death were on every side.

And what weird uniforms they wore. Some none at all. No two men in the whole band were dressed exactly alike. Some had the "guerrilla shirt" made of fine material and painstakingly sewed by wives and sweethearts; some had on anything they could find in the barrel. All, however, more or less agreed in one respect: they wore wide belts, with pistols jammed into them. Some had four pistols, and also carried a rifle. Some had two rifles fastened to their saddles. They had arms and ammunition and they were aching to put them to use.

They rode along the Oregon Trail where the covered wagons had once creaked—the very trail the Donner Party had followed. They arrived at Gardner, Kansas, at eleven o'clock at night and turned north toward Lawrence. The town's fate was sealed.

The night was dark; they had to have guides, so Quantrill would rap at a farmer's door and order him to guide them. After a time, in the darkness, the farmer would become hazy as to directions. "Is this as far as you know the country?" Quantrill would ask.

"Yes," the farmer would say thankfully.

"Then you can go home."

As the man turned to walk away, Quantrill would shoot

him. Then Quantrill would rap on another door. That night eight farmers were killed.

When they got to the edge of the town, the sun was as high as a tree. Quantrill signaled for his men to gather around. He thought they might not get his orders just right, so he told the men again: "Kill every man and burn every house." He was a perfectionist. They rode quietly until they saw a Negro preacher in the barnyard milking. It was his end; the cow went crippling away. They came to a tent camp of twenty-two raw Federal recruits who were just waking up. In three minutes eighteen of them were dead. And now, giving the Rebel yell, Quantrill's men, in columns of fours, started down the streets of the town, firing right and left.

The hated Jim Lane—he was a United States senator and the most important man in Kansas—heard the firing, leaped out of bed, rushed outside, and tore his nameplate off the door—quick thinking, indeed. In his nightshirt he ran into a field where the August corn was as high as his head and sped to a farmer's where he borrowed trousers, shoes, a hat, mounted a plowhouse, and escaped, thus defeating a key purpose of Quantrill's murderous march.

George A. Collamore, the mayor, heard shouts and, going to the window, saw men in the street. Hastily slipping out the back door, he climbed down into the well which was near the house. It was a "rock well," made of rough, jutting rocks on which he could get a toehold; by propping himself against the side of the well, he could keep his position fairly safely. The guerrillas demanded to know where he was; his wife said he was out of town. Enraged because they hadn't captured the mayor, they set the house on fire. As it was burning, the mayor's wife went to the rear, where the well was, and called down. Her husband answered and she left. The guerrillas remained until the house was consumed, then departed. As soon as they had gone, the mayor's wife went to the well. The heat had drawn the air out, heavy gases had settled into the well, and the mayor's body was floating on the water, dead from asphyxiation.

The men prided themselves on how many they had killed. Bloody Bill claimed to have killed fourteen, and the count was allowed. That many more knots in his delicate silken string.

One of the most ruthless was Cole Younger, who burned and shot and killed like a madman. But he met with an unexpected turn. Entering a house, he found a man hiding in a closet. Cole yanked him out. "Please don't kill him," cried the wife. "He has asthma."

"Has asthma?" repeated the startled Cole.

"Yes. He has it so bad that he hasn't slept in a bed for nine years."

"I wouldn't kill anyone with asthma," said Cole, and left the house, the man wheezing his thanks.

This curious and unpredictable character showed another side of himself that day. With four men Cole entered a house where they found three old men, none in uniform, none of war age. Cole's companions wanted to kill the three at once, but Cole would not have it and made his men come out of the house with him. Then he left one of his men to guard the house and continued on down the street on his grim errand. Yes, a strange man.

The town was burning. Drunken men staggered up and down the streets, a bottle in one hand, a pistol in the other, emptying both. They blazed away at anything or anybody who looked like a Jayhawker, Quantrill's orders forgotten. If it moved, kill it.

Quantrill had been working hard and was hungry. He went to the City Hotel, and ordered breakfast; he said he had boarded here when he had been in Lawrence and knew that it set a good table. He ate quietly, disturbed only by the rifle fire and the smell of burning buildings. After the meal he felt much better and went back to work.

He got himself a team of white horses and a buggy and rode up and down the streets inspecting the fruits of his victory.

In four hours it was all over. One hundred and eighty-three men and boys were dead, but not a woman had been harmed; the guerrillas were gallant men and believed in the nobility of womanhood.

It was almost noon. Quantrill and his men must move and move fast, for the Federal troops would soon be upon them. And the Federal troops soon were, but the wily Quantrill escaped. He gave orders for his troops to break up into small detachments, and this they did.

Four or five months later Quantrill himself, with a faithful few, crossed the Mississippi River into Kentucky, where he thought he would be safe. He was mistaken, for the Union troops found him and killed him in a cow lot.

His troops never rode again as a unit in Missouri or Kansas. His triumph at Lawrence was the end of Quantrill and his death machine.

Quantrill was Cole's tutor. Cole took an advanced course under Bloody Bill Anderson, and some special homework from George Todd, who could barely read and write but who was a genius in his own line.

The raid was not all death and disaster; now and then there was a lighter touch. I found such an item in the *Independence Examiner* for August 22, 1941, in the form of an interview with G. B. Cummings of Blue Springs, Missouri. In his youth he had known a printer who had been employed on the *Kansas Weekly Tribune* at the time of the raid. This is the story the printer told:

He was sleeping above the printshop when, about dawn, he was awakened by rifle shots. He dressed hurriedly, and ran down the front stairs and into the street. Someone shouted to him that the Missouri guerrillas were sacking and burning the town. The printer ran back into the building and down a rear stairway. As he stood in the back yard hesitating what to do, he heard a squad of soldiers coming down the street, firing and yelling. The printer had to act fast. A printer can do that, as all ex-newspapermen know.

In this yard also was a "rock well." He started down the well, holding on as best he could. He stayed about an hour. The firing squad went by. Now he could come up. Before he started, he took out his wallet and stuck it among the rocks. Finally he reached the top, exhausted but safe. The guerrillas had all gone and the town was beginning to feel at ease. The printer returned to the well but felt too exhausted to climb down again, so he asked a young fellow to go for him. This the young man did, finally arriving back at the top with the wallet safely in his pocket. The printer then paid the young man the sum the two had agreed upon, $2.50. The purse contained $8.00.

CHAPTER IV

Cole Meets Jesse James for the First Time. Also Meets Myra Belle Shirley for the First Time

WITH the fall apart of Quantrill's men, Cole and his company started for Texas in the fall of 1863. At this very time a girl, four years younger than Cole, was also going to Texas—Myra Belle Shirley, who was to flash across the sky as Belle Starr. The two had been born within about one hundred miles of each other but had never heard of each other. Now they were going to the same general section of Texas.

Cole was to report to General Benjamin McCulloch at Bonham, and there Cole went, glad, no doubt, to get out of Hell's Corner. He was a captain and was important enough to order supplies from the commissary and the quartermaster department by signing the slips with his name with C. S. A. after it.

In November 1863 he was sent to Shreveport, Louisiana, where he and his company were to try to capture cotton growers who were selling their product to Union forces. Five miles from Tester's Ferry, on Bayou Macon, he and his men met a wagon train loaded with cotton, convoyed by fifty cavalrymen. Cole and his men far outnumbered the cotton guards and charged them at full gallop, giving the Rebel yell that Cole had so often screeched in Missouri and Kansas. When the affair was over, forty of the cotton men were dead. But this was not quite all. Cole found four men following close behind the wagon train. Cole questioned them and discovered they were cotton buyers; they were searched, and $180,000 found. That settled their fate. On the way Cole had passed a cotton gin; taking the unhappy four back to the gin, he hanged them then and there. He sent the money to Bastrop, Louisiana, to be used by the Confederacy. He was honest in the handling of the money, making no effort to keep any for himself. At this time Cole was meticulously honest.

A few days later, at Bayou Monticello, he came upon another cotton train. He had better luck here, killing fifty-two men; no hangings. He made two more charges, one at Goodrich's Landing, the other at Omega. Cole was King Cotton. In fact, he was so successful that he was sent on a foray into Arkansas, coming back with blood on his hands and bay leaves in his hair. Everything was going his way.

He had an easy time during the winter of 1863–64, no hiding in the hollows. Many Missourians had fled to Texas, some to save their property, some their necks. No Union forces to make life unpleasant. The Missourians in this new land began to visit back and forth. There was quite a little group of Missourians around a settlement named Scyene (pronounced Sie-een), ten miles east of Dallas. One of the Missourians who had arrived there was John Shirley, a hotel-keeper from Carthage. He had a brother on a farm near Scyene, and a son, Preston Shirley, living north of Dallas. With John Shirley was his daughter, Myra Belle Shirley, sixteen years old. The Shirley family had driven by covered wagon all the way from Carthage—quite a jaunt. On the way they had passed the South Canadian River in the Indian Territory and a crookneck later famous as Younger's Bend. Myra Belle saw the place with her own eyes, but it wasn't named then. She hit on the idea herself, later. Cole Younger himself never dreamed that he would have a section of a river named in his honor. Later he wished he hadn't had.

One day Cole happened to be near Scyene and decided to call on his fellow Missourians. His fate was twisted then and there.

The Shirley family was glad to welcome Cole and he was invited to dinner. John Shirley had never heard of Cole, but Cole had heard of the Shirley Hotel in Carthage. The two knew people in common, and conversation crackled along delightfully. Now and then Cole glanced at Myra Belle, and now and then Myra Belle glanced at the visitor. What she saw was pleasing: a handsome young man lacking half an inch of being six feet, with blue eyes, brown hair, and a complexion that was light for one who had slept outdoors so much in all kinds of weather. And he had a pleasant, engaging manner. Besides all this, he was a captain in the Confederate Army. Myra Belle found him interesting.

What the young captain saw was a fairly good-looking girl of sixteen with unusually black hair and black eyes. She didn't have to be too ravishing to intrigue Cole, who had seen few girls since he had taken to the brush. Cole found her definitely interesting.

At last he rode away and that, seemingly, was the end of the matter.

In May 1864 Cole, under the command of Colonel George S. Jackson, went with a detachment to Colorado to cut the international telegraph line running from Leavenworth, Kansas, to San Francisco. The line was cut and then Cole, with his company, heard that a Federal wagon train was lumbering across Colorado. He rushed out to take it. But the wagon train was empty and there was nobody to kill. It was disappointing.

Cole was sent to Mexico; on the way he had a bout with the Comanches. From brush fighting to Indian fighting—quite a jump! It shows how varied America was, and how unsettled the times. The boy was making a career of fighting, but so were many other young men who had lived along the border between Missouri and Kansas.

He got as far as Guaymas, Mexico, accomplishing nothing. Here he found something new. The Confederacy had bought two ships from the British; these were to be delivered at Victoria, British Columbia. Somebody had to go there to take them over. Cole was one of five men assigned. The five disguised themselves as American miners who had been working in Mexico and who were on their way to California to have a go at gold. When they got to California they would proceed to Victoria. They set out by stage and everything went nicely—except that when they got to Victoria they found that General Lee had surrendered and the war was over.

It will be remembered that his first engagement had been at Carthage, Missouri, July 5, 1861, so he had been in the saddle four years. The boy had been seeing life—and death.

This is Cole's war record:

At seventeen in his first battle.

At seventeen joins Quantrill.

At seventeen kills his first man.

At eighteen sworn into the Confederate Army.

At eighteen made a lieutenant.

At eighteen a price on his head of $1,000.

At nineteen a captain.

At nineteen in the Lawrence raid.

All this while he was still of school age.

His was a more dramatic case than most, but there were other boys who were having experiences almost as extraordinary.

He himself had lived through the war, but things hadn't gone well with some of his tutors. Quantrill, after having been wounded in the cow lot, had died in a hospital in Louisville, Kentucky, and was put into a grave that soon became unidentifiable. Bloody Bill Anderson was having a tough time, too, for he had been shot to shreds.

The writer was shown Anderson's grave by Elmer L. Pigg, the authority on Anderson. Bloody Bill was killed and was buried in Richmond, Missouri—curiously enough only a few feet from where the first Mormon martyrs were buried. There is no chain, fence, or even post to separate the heroic Mormon men from Missouri's worst killer. The grave is unmarked and can be seen only by someone who knows its location.

George Todd died with his cavalry boots on, too. Two of Cole's saddle companions, however, were still kicking: Frank James and George Shepherd.

Cole visited an uncle in Los Angeles, then started home by stage, no minor now. How peaceful it would be to be at home! He was twenty-one and was just starting out in life. He had killed many men and had been wounded twenty times. But all this in the line of duty. He had never stolen a cent and he never dreamed he would become an outlaw. In fact, it was still in his mind to become a farmer, as most men were in these days.

In the fall of 1865 he reached the old farm where he was born. His brother Jim had joined Quantrill just in time to be captured in the cow lot and had been clapped into a Federal prison at Alton, Illinois. Now the war was over and he had been released, getting back to the farm the same week that Cole arrived. It was a rather touching family re-union. Bob, Cole's younger brother, was there; and so was

John, the youngest of all. Also there was Suse, the family servant, who had endured such shocking treatment from the Jayhawkers. But Cole's mother wasn't well; nor had she been since she had had to set her own house on fire and ride the eight miles through the snow. Those, indeed, were rugged days.

But now all that foolishness was over. The dove of peace had returned with a sprig of green in its mouth.

Instead of good times, conditions shortly proved to be almost as bad as ever. The bitterness between the Northern and the Southern ex-soldiers had grown instead of waning. The fact that someone had signed some papers down in Virginia made little difference in Missouri. The Kansas Jayhawkers meant to get even with the Missouri bushwhackers. And the Missouri bushwhackers meant to wring the neck of every Jayhawk they saw. Death, rapine, and murder stalked the roads; no traveler was safe; if he had money, it made little difference which side he was on. Pockets were turned wrong side out, a search was made for money belt—then a hasty grave under the leaves.

The Judy incident popped up. It will be remembered that Judy's son had been killed and that the father had blamed Cole. When matters couldn't be any worse, they promptly deteriorated: Judy, the father, was elected sheriff in the county next to the one where Cole had come home. Judy had no rights in the county, but this made no difference to Judy, who gathered a posse around him and started for the Younger home. Cole had to take to the brush again. It was like old times. Judy and his handymen searched the house. When they couldn't find Cole, they made the faithful Suse cook them a midnight supper, then they got into their saddles and rode into the night.

Now and then Cole would go home; soon he would have to disappear. Southern ex-soldiers couldn't preach or teach, or practice law, or even be justices of the peace without taking the "Iron-clad Oath." If anyone gave a meal or a night's lodging to a bushwhacker he could be thrown into jail. The list of things a Southerner couldn't do was long and impressive. Liberty, Missouri, which was in the thick of it, felt such great resentment against the North that the Confederate flag was flown over the courthouse until the latter part of 1869. The land itself was a widespreading weed patch. Lone, gaunt chimneys stood where houses once had looked across the meadows. In fact, the land was so desolate that the deer had returned; wild turkeys gobbled in trees. There was no money; people returned to barter, as their ancestors had done in the early days—a dozen eggs for a pound of coffee.

Cole had no horses and no implements. What was he to do?

In January 1866 something happened that changed his life. He rode over to Kearney, Missouri, to visit his old friend and saddle companion, Frank James.

"I want you to meet my brother Jesse," said Frank. "In the family we call him Dingus."

Cole saw a rather handsome boy with a faintly turned up nose, brown hair, blue eyes, high cheekbones, and the tip of the third finger on his left hand shot off.

"He's kind of poorly," continued Frank. "He picked up a couple of lung shots April 23, 1865, when he was coming into the Burns schoolhouse to surrender. Wasn't that a piece of luck—to be wounded by the Feds when he was on the way in to surrender! But he's a lot better now; in fact, gets around pretty lively. Couldn't ride horseback for quite a while, but now he's all right in the saddle again."

Cole looked down with kindly condescension on Jesse. Cole himself was a veteran of four years of knocking men out of the saddle. Jesse had been in the business only half a year. On top of this Cole was twenty-two; Jesse eighteen and a half —a chasm.

Cole knew Jesse was tough, but he didn't realize how tough he was, or how tough he could get. Jesse had been receiving plenty of training under Bloody Bill Anderson, and at the dreadful Centralia Massacre young Jesse had cruelly killed Major A. E. V. Johnson. Jesse was bad medicine.

They talked about how hard times were and how impossible it was to get started farming and, as they talked, an idea developed: that they could stop some of the travelers going through this section and get money. The thought was not shocking to any of the three; they had been used to taking money from people all during the war. This had been done in the cause of war, but civilians as well as soldiers had been relieved of their money. Cole mentioned his own father. But robbing a traveler was small pickings; some travelers didn't have enough to shoe a mule. Why not do it in a bigger way? Rob a bank! The idea was breathtaking.

Everybody hated banks; they were unregulated; they charged usury; they cheated farmers in freight rates and on land deals. Some people had lost their savings in wildcat railroad stocks. A farmer felt that when he got into the clutches of a bank, he was a gone gosling. In no time at all the bank would have his farm and he would be in a covered wagon going up and down the country trading horses with gypsies. So great was the feeling against banks that bankers were cursed on the streets.

No bank in America had ever been robbed by force of arms, except during the Civil War, when, in October 1864,

Rebel troops descended on St. Albans, Vermont, helped them-selves to the money, and fled across the line into Canada where, for the time being, they were safe from the irate Northerners.

Little by little the three worked out the idea. But which bank? The bank at Liberty, Missouri, was only a few jumps from the James homestead and not far from Cole's home near Lee's Summit. That was it!

Whom would they take? That was a minor matter; there were plenty of bushwhackers Frank and Cole knew who were dependable men. After the robbery they would separate, as Quantrill had taught them, and disappear into the brush like quail. Why, said the men, growing enthusiastic, it was a fine idea. Seize the money and vamoose.

It would take quite a few, but the men were available; most of them were ex-guerrillas and were not squeamish about seeing a man double up with his hand on his stomach. Jesse was filled with excitement; he would like to go, but the gunshot wounds were a trouble, damn it. He would have to stay at home with the women. It was humiliating.

And so on February 13, 1866, twelve men on horseback rode into Liberty, Missouri, where the Confederate flag was flying over the courthouse. They rode in quietly from two directions, and no one paid any attention to the casual horse-men. Suddenly one of them gave a signal and the twelve gave the terrifying Rebel yell and charged down the street, shoot-ing right and left. Three of the men rushed into the bank and came out with $57,072.64—a nice morning's work. This was not only the first civil bank robbery, but it also marked the debut of that sturdy character, the grain sack. The grain sack became famous; no bank, stagecoach, or train after that was ever robbed without the grain sack doing its bit. Everything went smoothly, except that a student at William Jewell College was killed. The men galloped out of town and disappeared. Not one of them was ever arrested, not one went to jail. It was heady stuff.

After things cooled down, Frank James came home and told Jesse about it. It made Jesse's tongue hang out.

Cole Younger didn't know it, that bright February morning, but the course of his life had been changed.

He had a problem on his hands. He was the best-known individual in the group. He had gained some fame in this section of Missouri where the people were proud of him and where many knew him by sight. He would have to get out, and get out fast. And he did exactly that. He set out on horseback for Texas. The distance now on horseback would be tremendous, but at that time men thought little of riding 800 miles. Sometimes they slept on the ground; sometimes they went to a tavern; sometimes, if the tavern was filled, they slept in its hallway or in its parlor.

Family affection was deep in Cole; he loved his mother, he cherished the memory of his father, and he considered himself the protector of his three brothers, who could plenty well take care of themselves. There was not much chance for them to get started in farming or in business in Missouri, so he gathered his three brothers around him—Jim, John, and Bob—in that age order. What a safari they made as they rode toward the sunny Southland. And what mischief they were to perpetrate.

Cole went to Tensas Parish, to the Amos Farm on what was known as Fortune Creek, where he hid. Everything was as peaceful as wind on the grass. If any Missourian wanted Cole's scalp, he did not come for it. On top of this, Cole had plenty of money—a fabulous amount for an ex-bushwhacker.

He remained three months, then went to East Carroll

Parish, Lake Providence, to what was known as the Bass Farm, where he settled down again. For years he had led an exciting life; now he had nothing to do and plenty of time to do it in. He began to think about the good Missourians he had met at Scyene, and got on his horse again.

CHAPTER V

Belle Starr Becomes a Spy for the Bushwhackers. She Meets Cole Younger. Cole Makes Mysterious Trips North

To GET A full grasp of the amazing career of Cole Younger I'll have to tell something about the early life of Belle Starr. She was born on a farm twelve miles northwest of Carthage, Missouri, February 3, 1848. (It is interesting to note that George Washington Carver, the Negro scientist, was also born on a farm twelve miles from Carthage—however, in another direction. There is a marker on the farm where he was born, none on Belle's. Two contrasting careers, indeed!) Belle always said that the place of her birth was Carthage, but her father did not move there until she was six or seven years old. For that matter, it wasn't much of a place to move to—only about three hundred people lived there. Her father, when he moved, gave up farming and started a hotel. The following advertisement appeared in the *Carthage Southwest Times* for March 29, 1861:

CARTHAGE HOTEL
North Side Public Square
John Shirley, Proprietor
Horses and Hacks to Hire. A good stable attached.

In addition John Shirley owned a livery stable and the buildings on the north side of the public square. He was well to do for the time and period. He was never, as some writers have set down, known as "Judge" Shirley. He was just plain John Shirley, a hustler and a rather likable fellow. Among his sons were Preston and another, known in the family as "Bud." Myra Belle was younger than either of these.

Belle went to school upstairs on the square and, later, to the Carthage Female College, where she took music and learned to play the piano. Judged by the standards of the time she was "cultivated." She was fairly good-looking, with unusually dark hair and eyes, and had a jolly personality—except when she got mad. The people who remembered her from this period said that the transformation was startling. Even the boys in school were afraid of her when she got into a temper. When her flare-up was over, she could again be a pleasant and agreeable companion.

She had learned to shoot and handle firearms while she was still on the farm; and now, in town, she continued to ride and shoot. Her father, naturally, had plenty of horses and soon Myra Belle was considered a good rider and shot. Sometimes the travelers at the hotel would watch her as she mounted a horse and rode harum-scarum down the street, popping away at nothing, just for the fun of it. Her father was proud of her; she was a bit "wild," but she would get over it.

She grew up a "model young lady"—except for her temper fits. The Border War between Missouri and Kansas was raging; this turned into the Civil War and, although only a young girl, Belle was drawn into it. Girls were extensively used as informers, and a spy job came to Belle. The story of what happened has become one of the most hotly contested stories in her life. It is "The Major Eno Story." It first appeared in a Richard K. Fox publication and was made up out of whole cloth. Later, in 1898, the story was taken up by

S. W. Harman in his *Hell on the Border* and passed along
to more thrilled customers. In fact, Harman's chapter dealing with this incident has been put into book form; you can
buy it down at the drugstore. It's exciting reading; the only
catch is that it's not true. When Harman wrote about Hanging Judge Parker's court, he was good, for he was a lawyer
in the court; when he got outside the court, he was a child.
And he got outside when he wrote about Belle's early days;
he knew nothing about them and never bothered to look
them up.

The true story comes, I think, from Mrs. Louise Brock
Murphy, Neosho, Missouri. Her family came into this
section of the Ozarks in 1833 when the Osage Indians were
there, and she has lived in the county all her life. Her family
knew the Shirleys. She and her husband Ralph bought the
old house and were restoring it when I visited them. It is
known as the Richey Mansion House and is the very building where Belle Starr made a bit of history. The location of
Mansion House is in Newtonia. The porches and wide
verandas were shot off during the war and have not yet been
restored. The restoration work so far has all been inside;
soon it will move outside. One cannon ball is still in the wall
of the ancient house, from which it peeps out like a bird from
its nest. The story was told to me by Mrs. Murphy. It, in
turn, was told to her by Mrs. Mildred Graves Sanders who
was the daughter-in-law of the man who built the house—
Matthew H. Richey. The story has been handed down in the
Richey family for years.

Mr. Richey was a Union man and was in the habit of
sheltering Union soldiers and sympathizers. One evening in
February 1863 Richey and his family were surprised to see
a girl of about fifteen ride up in front of the house and
calmly dismount at the horse block. She tied her horse, and

started for the door. By this time the house was agoggle. A young and unaccompanied girl!

"My name is Myra Belle Shirley and I live in Carthage," she said smoothly. "I've been visiting friends and got lost on my way back. Can I stay overnight?"

Of course she could stay overnight, said unsuspecting Mr. Richey.

She was taken up to what was called the "black bedroom," this because everything in it was painted that color. She had supper with the Richeys, talking pleasantly with them. The Richey family knew the Shirley family in Carthage, but did not like them. However, they liked Belle, who was making herself so agreeable. All eyes were on her as she chatted, girl-like, about nothing.

One of the guests staying in the house was Major Edwin B. Eno, of the 8th Missouri Militia, a cavalry regiment. This meant that he was a Union man.

After supper the people went into the parlor where there was a square rosewood grand piano. Belle obligingly sat down and played. Everybody thought this was delightful. After the music she again talked pleasantly, now and then asking a question. The sum and substance of these questions had to do with the Union troops and how many were there. She learned also that the Richey house was being used as headquarters for Major Eno and his officers, that enlisted men were using the stone barn and the stone mill as barracks; in addition, some of the men were encamped in the town of Newtonia. Belle smiled brightly; it was interesting to know such things, she said.

The next morning she came down to breakfast early and again was pleasant and agreeable and most appreciative of the hospitality that had been extended her. After breakfast she said she would have to get home as fast as she could so that her parents would not worry about her. Her horse was saddled and brought.

"I want to get some switches for my horse," said Belle. With Mr. Richey's daughter she went to a clump of cherry bushes and cut off two or three. Then she walked slowly back to her horse, mounted the horse block, got into her side-saddle, and rode briskly off in the direction of Carthage.

She had gone only two or three miles when hell struck the Richey house. The cutting of the cherry switches had been a signal to Confederate lookouts who had been watching and who reported to their officers. A fusillade was launched against the house. It was such a spirited attack that Major Eno and his officers had to leave and could no longer use the house as officers' headquarters. It was quite a little victory for Belle.

Later there was a desperate battle at Newtonia and the room where Belle had slept was used as a hospital and in it two or three soldiers died. The room is no longer painted black and is called the Belle Starr Room. It contains none of the furniture it had when she was so entertaining to her host, but it does have the furniture of the period.

The foxy Fox writers seized upon the incident and improved on it. They thought that Belle had a twin brother Ed; well, it would be good readin' if she saved his life. In no time at all she saved his life, and a neat trick it was. Here's the way those creative artists had her do it:

On her fourteenth birthday, February 3, 1862, as Belle, returning from a scouting expedition, was riding through the village of Newtonia, in the eastern part of Newton County, Missouri, thirty-five miles from her home town, Carthage, she was intercepted by Major Eno, who, with a troop of cavalry, was stationed in the village and who had his headquarters in the home of Judge M. H. Richey.

On the day of Belle Starr's capture, Major Eno had sent a detachment of cavalry for the purpose of capturing her brother, Captain Shirley, who was known to be on a visit to his home. Myra, or Belle, as she was later called, had ridden into that section of the country for the purpose of obtaining information that might be of value to her people, and, having discovered that men had been sent to capture her brother, was on the point of hastening to warn him when she was arrested and detained, as mentioned above. She had been in the habit of riding recklessly where she pleased, and as scarcely any Union soldier would think of molesting a woman, especially when she chanced to be a beautiful and buxom one, her plans had not, hitherto, been disarranged. It happened that Major Eno, who had resided in Carthage, was acquainted with both her and her brother, as children, and this was why he had ordered her arrest, rightly surmising that she was about to go to her brother's assistance. The girl was taken to a chamber of the Richey house and guarded by the major himself, who laughed at her annoyance. This served to anger her and she gave expression to her rage in loud and deep curses. She would sit at the piano and rattle off some wild selection in full keeping with her fury; the next moment she would spring to her feet, stamp the floor, and berate the major with all the ability and profanity of an experienced trooper, while tears of mortification rolled down her cheeks, her terrible passion increased only by the laughter and taunts of her captor. At last, believing his men to have had plenty of time to reach Carthage, Major Eno said:

"Well, Myra, you can go now. My men will have your brother under arrest before you can reach him."

With eagerness trembling in every lineament, she sprang to the door, rushed to the stairway, and out to a clump of cherry bushes, where she cut several long sprouts.

The grave is unusual in that it has two stones; the smaller one was put up by the Confederate States of America. Cole was buried within five miles of where he was born.

The earliest known picture of Cole Younger, taken before he joined Quantrill (Cole, left; Jim on the right). This is the first publication of this picture.

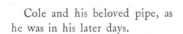

Cole and his beloved pipe, as he was in his later days.

From the Grinter Studio, Independence, Missouri

The last roll call of Quantrill's guerrillas, in September, 1920. They always put Quantrill's picture in the middle. The man on the first row, on the right, is Jesse James, Junior. The man on the left, front row, is Harry C. Hoffman, quoted in the book, but not a Quantrill rider. This is the first publication of this picture.

COLE YOUNGER

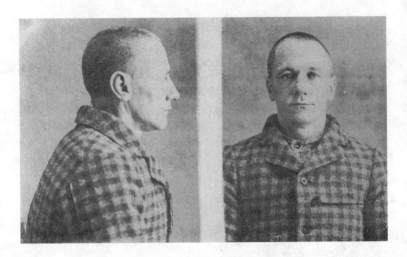

This is the way he looked when he went in—

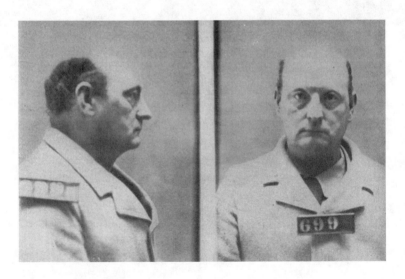

—and this is the way he looked when he came out.

Quantrill's raid on Lawrence, Kansas. The man with the up-raised gun is
Cole Younger. Cole was present at the sacking of Lawrence and killed
several men, but not in the manner shown.

Shooting of fifteen prisoners. This drawing and accompanying text, showing Cole firing at Federal prisoners, caused him endless trouble. He was not
present at the Centralia Massacre, which the picture purportedly depicts.

This rare photograph was believed to have been Belle Starr's outlaw home in Younger's Bend, but recently has been identified as the headquarters of the Hendrix & Royer Ranch in the Arbuckle Mountains in Oklahoma. Belle's place was much like the one shown in this picture.

Pearl Younger. This portrait has never before been published. She broke her mother's heart.

Belle Starr, from a portrait by Vincent R. Mercaldo.

This is the Cole Younger School, as it is usually called. Its official name is Younger's Bend School. It is near what was Belle Starr's Outlaw Heaven.

This set of bone furniture was made by firemen in St. Joseph, Missouri, in 1904. They admired Belle Starr so much they made this as a tribute to her. The set weighs nine hundred pounds.

Cole Younger's birthplace as it looks today. The lean-to has been added. The house is unusual in that it has three rooms below, six above.

Charlie Pitts, who was the roughest, crudest man in the outlaw band.

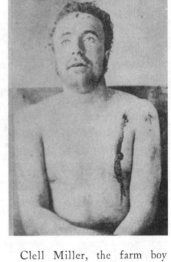

Clell Miller, the farm boy from Clay County, who joined the James-Youngers to "have some fun."

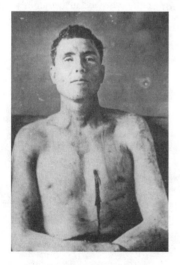

Bill Chadwell is the one who suggested the James-Youngers rob a Minnesota bank.

Bob Younger, Cole's baby brother. He was twenty-three when he rode forth that day.

Her horse stood just where her captors had left it. She vaulted into the saddle, and sped away, plying the cherry sprouts with vigor. She was a beautiful sight as she rode away through the fields, her lithe figure clad in a closely fitting jacket, erect as an arrow, her hair, unconfined by her broad-brimmed, feather-decked sombrero, falling free and flung to the breeze, and her right hand plying the whip at almost every leap of her fiery steed. The major seized a small field glass and, ascending to an upper room, watched her course across the great stretch of level country.

"Well, I'll be ——!" he ejaculated admiringly. "She's a born guerrilla. If she doesn't reach Carthage ahead of my troopers, I'm a fool."

The major was right: when his detachment of cavalry galloped leisurely into Carthage that evening they were greeted by a slip of a girl mounted on a horse. She dropped a curtsy and asked:

"Looking for Captain Shirley? He isn't here—left half an hour ago—had business up Spring River. 'Spect he's in Lawrence County by this time."

There is no proof that Major Eno ever tried to capture Bud Shirley, let alone so dramatically as in the Fox-Harman story. Shirley was not a captain, as most writers set him down, but a bushwhacker, and not a very courageous one at that. He was killed in 1863, at Sarcoxie, Missouri—shot in the back by Union soldiers when he was running away. But the story of Belle's daring ride is now as surrounded by legend as a hazelnut kernel by its shell and will probably endure forever.

"The Belle Starr House," as it is called, is on Highway 86, eleven miles from Highway 71. It will be recalled that the house where Cole Younger was born is on Highway 71. (Both houses are open to the public.)

Conditions in southwest Missouri grew steadily worse; no man, when he laid himself down at night, knew if he would wake in the morning. Southerners were hastily pulling out for Texas, where they would not have to deal with Union troops. One of the early ones to go was Preston Shirley, the oldest child. It was not long before he arrived at a wide place in the road called Scyene.

Now, after Bud's death, Mr. Shirley decided to go to Texas, too, and looked around for a buyer for his hotel, livery stable, and buildings. He was able to dispose of them and, late in 1863, put Mrs. Shirley and Myra Belle into a covered wagon and started on the long trek. On the way they passed the crookneck in the South Canadian River that Belle made famous as Younger's Bend.

They moved in with Preston, pretty well filling the place. Mr. Shirley began to farm, not too briskly; he just took his time about it, for he had plenty of money. Belle was put in a one-room district school where she looked down on the other students, for she had gone to a female seminary that had a great school bell and prayers every morning. To a girl who had once been a spy, life was exceedingly slow-paced. Worst of all, there seemed to be no escape. Milk, wash dishes, hoe in the garden. Could she ever stand it? One of her few pleasures was to ride her horse—which she did superbly—and to practice with her pistol. The rest of the time make beds, work in the garden, shuffle in to another monotonous meal. Not very exciting.

But one day life again became very exciting, indeed. Five men rode up to her father's cabin—by this time her father had built one of his own—and hallooed after the good old Missouri style. Her father went out and was delighted to find they were from Missouri. The leader was Cole Younger, whom Belle had met before. Two of the other riders were his brothers, almost as rugged as Cole himself was.

"Come in, Cole," said Mr. Shirley warmly. "Glad to see you again."

Cole went in and greeted the family.

"You remember my wife Eliza," said John Shirley.

"Howdy do, Miz Shirley," said Cole.

"And my daughter Belle."

"I'm pleased to meet you again," said Cole warmly.

Cole was now twenty-two. Myra Belle was eighteen.

"I'm always pleased to meet anybody from home," said Cole. "I thought I'd ride over and say hello."

"I'm glad you did," said Belle in a notable understatement.

"Weren't you a captain under Quantrill?" asked Mr. Shirley.

"Yes. I was a captain at nineteen."

"I did a little spy work around Carthage," said Belle.

"Missouri girls really accomplished a great deal for us," said Cole. "A great deal," he added.

The conversation floated along. Now and then Cole and Belle looked at each other. Then Cole felt he should talk to "the old folks."

"Eliza," said Mr. Shirley after a time, "can't you shake up a dinner for the boys?"

"I'll help," said Belle.

It was not long before the first table was served; all now felt at ease and exchanged war experiences. There were stories of the dreadful aftermath of the war when no Southerner was treated fairly. Cole was particularly vocal about this, for something was on his mind. In this aftermath he had, much to his astonishment, become an outlaw. Maybe, if he had been treated differently, he would be in Missouri, farming. Someday—when "things cleared up"—he would be. He'd buy a farm in Jackson or Cass County and "settle down." Nearly everybody was a farmer; he would be one. It was the way to live. The slaves his father had had were gone—all except old Suse. He would hire colored men to work for him. He would become an important man, like his father. Maybe a mail contractor. Why, it was four years since his father had been killed. But his mother was living. She was in "poor health" since she had been forced to set her own house on fire and travel through the snow. But it was something to have one's mother. As soon as he could he would go to Missouri and see her.

It was nice to talk to Belle Shirley about the fine state of Missouri. It'd certainly been rough going there for a while. Well, the North had won. One must make the best of it. Quantrill was dead. Jim Lane, the Red Leg, had shot himself. That was good. General Sterling Price was in poor health. That was bad. Frank James was still living and so was George Shepherd—two good men. A new man was being talked about—Buffalo Bill who was two years younger than himself and who had ridden with Jennison in Kansas, but was now hunting buffaloes for a railroad. Maybe one of the buffaloes would get him. Hope so. Meantime, it was nice, from time to time, to glance at Belle.

And Belle, on her part, was tremendously impressed. Why, in Texas, it was life among the lowly. Now a handsome captain had come. And he seemed to have money.

The day wore on.

"I wish I could ask you to stay overnight, but our quarters are a bit crowded," said Mr. Shirley.

"We've got blankets and are used to sleeping out," said Cole.

"It's not cold down here in Texas, like it is in Missouri," said Belle.

The men stayed two days, visiting with their new Missouri friends. It was nice to talk to home folks.

It was not long until Cole was back—alone this time. He and Belle began to ride together and to shoot at targets and at everything that popped up. He told of his adventures during guerrilla days. She listened raptly. To ride with Quantrill. Not only that, but to be a captain in his company! Never had she known such a wonderful, such a dashing, such a handsome man.

Belle's father grew uneasy. The reports on Belle's new friend were not too favorable. He was spending a great deal of time in the gambling houses in Dallas. Where did he get so much money? He had come out of the Civil War impoverished; now he had enough to fling around.

But he didn't drink. That was in his favor.

Mr. Shirley asked Preston to "talk" to Belle. Preston got nowhere. Belle and Cole continued to ride together. Sometimes he took her to Dallas and showed her its wonders.

One day Cole had bad news. He had to go "up No'th" on a business trip. Soon there were stories in the papers of a bank robbery and soon the debonair Cole came riding back. He'd seen his mother, he said; she was still suffering from the way the Feds had treated her. He had even more money now.

It was not long before Cole had to go North again. He would go and he would return, telling hardly anything at all about where he had been, or what he had seen, but to Belle he still seemed wonderful.

The mysterious trips continued.

Mrs. Shirley began to suspect something else, as she watched her daughter. Her suspicions turned out to be correct. Mr. Shirley was in a rage, but there was nothing he could do. And so, in the Shirley home, in 1869, a child was born and named Pearl Younger.

And there Cole came to live—the dashing captain who had arrived that memorable day three years before. But now there were no war tales; only ill feeling and bitterness. However, on the prairies, among scattered neighbors, not too much was thought about a new child appearing on the scene. The country was filled with rough men who had "gone to Texas," men who didn't ask foolish questions.

Cole began more and more to stay in Dallas. And to gamble more and more. Now and then he came back to see little Pearl; and each time he came Belle was delighted. He was still her hero.

One day Cole rode up hastily, swung off his horse, and came immediately into the house. "I got into a bit of trouble in Dallas, Belle."

"What kind of trouble, Cole?" asked the alarmed girl.

"I got into a gun fight and shot a man. He's not dead yet, but they're after me and I'll have to leave the country."

"Where are you going?"

"To Missouri. My friends will take care of me till this blows over."

"I'll go with you, Cole."

"You'll do no such thing," said her father. The sooner she got shut of this man the better, he told himself.

"I'm going with Cole," she said, and she did, against the protests of both her father and mother, and she took little Pearl.

Care of the child was a problem, so it was decided that Belle and the child should stay at a town in Texas until Cole could send for them. And then in a dramatic and touching scene Cole rode away. And Belle, looking after him, had faith in him. He would return. All would be well.

Her father learned that Belle was still in Texas and sent word that her mother was ill. Belle hurried back, to find that she had been tricked. Her mother was well. Belle, furious with her father, said that she would go to Missouri with the money Cole had given her. Her father was so enraged that he forced Belle to go upstairs, then told her that if she tried to get away he would take the child. The prospect of such action was too much for Belle and there, in semi-imprisonment, she remained.

She was young, her father said; she should go to school, and he asked her to go to a nearby school in the next county. She agreed, for she wanted to get out of the home filled with discord, but she had to leave her daughter. Belle was not happy in her school, thinking of Cole and little Pearl.

One day Cole rode up to the school. Belle could hardly believe her eyes, but there he was. She tried to keep this from the school, but soon all knew, and before the staring, incredulous students Belle got on the extra horse Cole had brought along and the two went flying away.

"You will stay with me," said Cole as the horses pounded down the road. "I've got friends who will take care of us."

If Belle had known who the friends were she might have been alarmed, for they were Cole's two brothers, Jim and Bob, Arch Clements, who had led the Liberty bank robbery, Allen Parmer, and Jesse and Frank James—the most deadly outlaws who had ever assembled in the United States. But Belle knew nothing of this and rode happily beside Cole.

Belle had known only guerrillas who were rugged, but now she was going among men who were even more rugged. They had money, and they were willing to spend it. They loafed on the farm Cole had rented. They went to Dallas and to the gambling rooms; when they came back they told of the hands they had held and how much they had won or lost.

The carefree, spendthrift life appealed to Belle. She was the center of attention. She had to cook but she made a lark of it; sometimes one of the men would be designated to cook. The men made a great many jokes about this. The men would come swaggering in and sit down at the table, all in good humor, all making jokes. During the meal there would be storytelling and laughter.

Now and then there would be a hint of danger. One of the men had "seen" somebody in Dallas. Their voices would grow low. In a few moments the conversation would leap up again.

Sometimes Belle would go to her father's home to see little Pearl. Her heart was touched, but her father was so bitter that she hated to have him come into the room where she was holding Pearl.

"You're mixed up with a bunch of outlaws and you're going to pay for it bitterly," he would say.

"It's better to be with them than in this house," she would reply.

After a time she would kiss the child good-by and return to the men.

She noted that the men were becoming secretive; their loud, boisterous laughter was gone. When they wanted to talk they went out to the barn where they would squat on their haunches, talking in low voices and punching their knives in the ground.

"Belle," said Cole, "I've got to leave you for a spell. I've got to go up No'th."

She trembled at the dire news. "You're not going off and leave me, are you?" she managed to say.

"Yes, Belle. I've got to go."

"You'll be back, won't you, Cole?" she cried.

"I'll be back just as soon as I can," he said.

In a few days Cole and the others mounted their horses and rode off. Belle stood watching until they were out of sight, then got on her own horse and started off to her father's house where little Pearl was.

CHAPTER VI

Rivalry for the Leadership of the
Gang Develops Between Cole and
Jesse James. The Incident at
Silas Hudspeth's

At first the people in Missouri had not associated Captain
Cole with the Liberty visit, but evidence began to accumulate.
Could it be possible that a man who had fought so nobly for
the South was now robbing right and left? Had the people
known it, this was the very matter that had made Cole a
robber; he had slipped, by easy stages, from guerrilla warfare into outlawry. Until Liberty, he had never stolen a cent.

Jesse James had joined the fearsome band. His wounds
had healed enough for him to hop a horse. He had a dual
personality. In his everyday comings and goings he was a
peaceful, likable citizen; he even had a sense of humor. But
when his will was pitted against another's, he was ruthless.
In the closing days of the Civil War he had seen blood and
carnage, and thought no more of killing a man than knocking
over a duck at a shooting gallery.

It soon became apparent that Jesse meant to be the leader.
He was the most desperate, the most fearless, the most bloodthirsty of the crew. His quick mind could conceive and out-
line a robbery better than anyone who had ever tried it in
the blood-soaked Middle West. However, it was not easy
sledding; some of the band thought that Cole was a good

man. He was older than Jesse, and far more experienced. One of the two would have to be the leader. The band could not have two heads.

Members of the James-Younger band were not "bad men" in the sense of the old-time West where the men were killers, swaggering up and down the streets, rolling into saloons, shooting out the lights, and having a good time in general. Sometimes the Western bad men took a dislike to some unhappy soul whose reflection they saw in a mirror and decided to do something about it. They were not robbers in the sense of holding up trains, stagecoaches, or banks; sometimes they helped themselves to the money on a faro table and departed into the night, their pockets bulging, their heels flying. But that was about all.

The James-Youngers were not this kind. They never shot out the lights, never took a drink at a bar, and never rode down the street shooting right and left for the heck of it. They were in the business of robbery and they stuck to their last. In fact, neither Jesse nor Cole, or for that matter Frank James, ever drank at all. Later, some of their "boys" did, but not the principals.

The topography of the country was just what the outlaws wanted—hardly any fences; of the few, many were stake-and-rider and could be flung down when the outlaws wished. They could cut across the country in almost any direction they chose; there were few bridges where officers of the law could lie in wait. An outlaw could ride ten miles from the scene of the robbery and be in Tibet, as far as people could tell. Even if a person saw a stranger who looked as if he might be on the scout, he kept his mouth shut—an excellent beauty hint. Not only did the topography favor the outlaws, so did their friends, many of whom had been under Quantrill; others, who had been in the Confederate Army, were willing to take The Boys in and feed and shelter them. For the most part, the outlaws were in clover. Now and then, however, a local man tattled; it was usually his swan song.

The men never hid in a cave and they never carried bedrolls, for the latter would mark them as riders who slept out at night—suspicious characters. Sometimes they slept in a barn, or in a schoolhouse, never in a cave, this despite the fact that there are ten caves in the United States that are pointed out as having housed the Jesse James gang. Instead, the men went to the best hotels, and well could they afford to, for they had the money. And they could order fancy meals. And when they went to a farmer's house and asked his wife to shake up a meal for them, they paid her handsomely. Once Cole handed a farmer's wife a five-dollar gold piece in payment for the dinner she had prepared for him. The woman almost fell against the stove.

How did Cole live during this period? This historian has no easy answer—or, for that matter, had the detectives who were after him month in and month out. Sometimes they thought they saw him, then he would vanish like Tinker Bell. Cole and the men did not ride together as a group; usually they rode in twos, at most in threes. They did not attract the attention that might be thought, for riders were constantly crossing and recrossing the country. Some were looking for land, some were legitimate cattle buyers. The pose of cattle buyer was made to order for Cole. A cattle buyer wore a long linen duster to keep off the dust and cattle grime. Cole found the garment admirably suited for hiding his personal effects. Besides, Cole looked like a cattle buyer. When he told a stranger that he was seeking cattle to buy, Cole was so convincing that you could hear a cow moo. And when he went into a bank and came out with a well-filled grain sack, you could hear the president bellow like a bull.

But Cole paid no attention to the man's distress, for by this time Cole would be pounding down the road, the grain sack balanced on his saddle, eager to get to Callaway County where he had as many friends as a wealthy widow.

A natural question is: How did they recruit their men? It wasn't so difficult as it might seem. The band was in its heyday of glory—the most feared outlaws who ever roamed the roads. Men wanted to join. When an aspirant turned up, Jesse or Frank James or Cole agreed to "talk" to him. These three usually knew the families of the men, at least something about them. Most of the new men were from Missouri. Two were from Kentucky, but they were cousins of the Jameses. So it was easy to know the man who was putting in his name. After a "talk" the new man would be told to come along. The band was, in truth, like a train: a man got on and rode a way and then got off; then somebody came and took his place. The train was rumbling along nicely. All was well.

Sometimes Cole wanted to get out of outlawry; he had got into it mainly by chance, for at bottom he was a reasonable man. But he was a cat on flypaper. When he raised one foot, the other sank into the mess. There was a reward on his head, dead or alive. He was not always certain who his friends were, who his enemies. One day as he and Frank James clopped along they talked about giving up the whole cursed thing, going to South America and "starting over." Easier said than done.

Often Cole thought of Belle Starr. She was the only woman who had come into his life. He hadn't been fair to her; he had left her with a child. As soon as he made a big haul he would go down to Texas, get Belle and baby Pearl, and go to the Pacific Northwest.

The Boys had robbed several banks in Missouri and were beginning to look around for new fields worthy of their talents. Cole suggested Kentucky, where no one knew them and where no bank in the state had ever been forcibly entered.

It wasn't long before Cole showed up alone at the bank in Russellville, Kentucky. Going to the cash window, he said, "I'm a cattle buyer from Louisville. Can you change a $100 bill for me?"

The cashier peered through the grillwork.

"My name is Colburn," Cole continued. "I may want to do business with your bank sometime." He was on solid ground there.

"I'm afraid I can't change your bill, Mr. Colburn," said the cashier.

With a look of pain on his face, Cole sadly returned the $100 bill to his pocket, then went slowly out, defeat and frustration in every step.

A week later Cole, accompanied this time by his friends, returned. The cashier was shocked to see Mr. Colburn once more at the window. But this time Mr. Colburn did not have a $100 bill in his hand; instead, he had something that looked as big as a cannon. "I'll take that money," said the hardhearted cattle buyer. He held out the sturdy grain sack.

Their bank business over, the men moved quickly to their horses, mounted, and went galloping down the street at a furious rate. The stunned citizens stood for some minutes, shaking the water out of their eyes, then organized a posse to chase the callers. They got on the work horses that were available and clopped after the Missouri men, not exactly eager to close with them, for the Kentucky men knew that the James-Younger men were dead shots, and did not pine to come to grips with them—a wise attitude. In fact, this attitude was a tremendous help to The Boys, as we called them in Missouri. Every posse knew it was dealing with the toughest men in America and so pursued the James-Younger gang at the pace of lame turtles.

The Boys got away without losing a man. They had scooped up $14,000.

What the happy and successful Boys didn't know was that Allan Pinkerton had been engaged to take them, dead or alive, and that Bloodhound Bligh was on their trail, nose to the ground, softly baying.

Cole had taken with him on this expedition his brother Jim, eager to learn the business. The boy showed promise and Cole was proud of him; he would go high in saddle circles. Also there was Cole's brother-in-law John Jarrette, an old hand at killing helpless men. He, too, showed promise. Also, come along for the ride, was George Shepherd and his brother Oll, short for Oliver. And Jim White, a young fellow who was just getting his working papers. All in all, they were a capable bunch, the best that America had yet turned out, bound to rise high in their specialty.

Cole liked to ride with his brothers, two of whom were now in business with him. John, the youngest, had been killed by a Pinkerton detective. Sometimes Cole and one of his brothers would pair up. He rode with Jesse James as little as possible; and when they had to talk to each other, their conversation was not on a diplomatic level. Cole never swore, but Jesse used the words that came handiest. On the other hand, Cole got along nicely with Frank James; the two had a deep regard for each other. Often they spoke of "the old days"—so far away did the guerrilla business seem. The sacking of Lawrence was only a memory. Time was moving along.

It was becoming more and more difficult for the James-Youngers; they had to ride farther and farther from home to earn a living. At about this time they heard of a fat goose in Iowa, in the little town of Corydon, a couple of jumps north of the Missouri-Iowa line, and decided to go there and pluck it. The word went out and they all got ready to make an Iowa visit. And this they did, not in a group but by twos —all eager to buy cattle. The seven horsemen arrived June 3, 1871, in Corydon—a day the town won't forget for years to come, so bizarre was what happened.

The town was "enjoying" a political fight; there is no other word for it. The matter had to do with the location of a new schoolhouse. One faction wanted it *here;* another faction wanted it *there.* The two rival factions were calling each other names that would shock sensitive readers. There was a "speaking" at the edge of town, and there the people stood, or sat, listening to the speakers tear into each other. They enjoyed the speaker when he was right and agreed with him; when he didn't agree with them, they said he didn't know what he was talking about. It was an old-time "town fight," pure and simple. And "simple" proved to be the exact word.

The seven Missouri cattle buyers arrived and rode leisurely down the street, looking as innocent as farm boys come to town on Saturday afternoon to stare into fascinating store windows.

One of the riders—it's not known which one—went into a bank with the tried and trusty $100 bill. Peering through the grillwork, he said, "Could you do me the favor of giving me change for this bill?"

"I'm afraid I can't, sir," said the cashier. "The treasurer of the bank is at the speaking, and he has the key to the safe."

"Is there some kind of meetin' goin' on?" asked the stranger, instantly interested in public affairs.

"It's a meeting about locating the new schoolhouse. I guess things are pretty lively over there. They've got an orator there named Henry Clay Dean who turns on the fireworks."

"I'd like to hear him," said the visitor sadly, "but I haven't got time. What can I do about this bill?"

"There's a new bank across the square," said the obliging cashier. "It might be able to take care of you. I hope so."

"I hope so, too," said the caller earnestly as he went out.

The visiting firemen held a hurried conference; then one of them walked across the square to the Obocock Brothers Bank and presented the faithful bill. "Could you oblige me by changing this?"

"Glad to," said the cashier, who wanted to build up good will for his bank. He turned and started to the safe to get the money. With the bills in his hand, he started back, and as he did so he saw something pointing at him as big as the end of a rain barrel.

"You make one false move and it will be the end of you," said the man behind the pistol. "Get into the back room and be quick about it."

The cashier followed the visitor's suggestion.

The men who had come into the bank, at a signal rushed into the back room, seized the cashier, and bound and gagged him. They began to toss all the available bills into the grain sack.

As they were busily at work, in walked a Negro preacher, prepared to make a deposit. He made it, but not in the way he had planned. One of the men held out the sack. "Throw it in here," said the heartless man. The preacher threw it in. But this was not all; he was ordered into the back room and tied and deposited beside the cashier. By this time all the available money had been picked up; the door to the back room was closed, and the seven horsemen started down the street with $40,000 in the bag, a nice morning's haul and not a single bit of unpleasantness.

As they rode along they came to the meeting at the edge of town. Henry Clay Dean, the spellbinder, was still holding forth. He had subtly switched the issue to politics, and was now giving the opposite party a drubbing.

Jesse James, who had a spark of humor in his lanky frame, stopped his horse at the edge of the crowd, listened a moment, then called out, "Excuse me for interruptin', but may I ask a question?"

"You may, my dear sir," called the orator, "and I shall endeavor to answer it to the best of my ability. Now, my friend, what is your question?"

"Did you know there's something wrong at the bank?"

"No, I didn't know it," said the ruffled man. "Is that the question you wanted to ask?"

"Yes," said Jesse. "That's the question."

The man frowned at the silly question.

"It's at the new bank," called the genial Jesse.

"Thank you," said the speaker dismissingly, and started to talk again.

Jesse turned and joined his fellow conspirators.

The orator started to get up steam after the singular interruption.

A man from the audience got up and began to edge out; it wouldn't hurt to look into the situation, his manner said. It wasn't long till the man came flying back. "The bank's been robbed!" he shouted.

That was the end of the speaking. The new schoolhouse would have to look after itself. Down the street as fast as they could pelt went the people. There, inside the bank, were the cashier and the preacher, working like mad to get free.

When they were released they gasped out what had happened.

Well, the farmers would capture the robbers and shoot them down like dogs. The farmers who had driven in for the speaking unhitched their horses and straddled them. The city people ran into the hardware store and came out with enough guns to supply a fort. The riders seized the guns, kicked their horses in the ribs, and started out of town on the trail of seven of the most dangerous men in America. Little by little the farmers began to think over what they were doing. Maybe they had better not ride so fast. And so, after the first brave show, they turned back and said the robbers had escaped them. The city people gathered around the men who had risked their lives and gazed at them admiringly.

Meanwhile the seven were riding gaily for Missouri, haven for the unappreciated.

The Pinkerton Detective Agency was notified and the son of the founder, Robert A. Pinkerton, took after the seven; he would soon have them inside looking out, he announced. That was the end of it. He followed them to Clay County, Missouri, and there the trail ended. In his report, Pinkerton said that the people in Clay and Jackson counties were willing to lie about the deplorable robbers. He gave it up and went back to Chicago, where people had a higher standard.

The Boys were now footloose again. They hadn't done so badly on their dip into Iowa. Forty thousand dollars was a lot of money, when you could buy a dinner at that time for a quarter.

These are the men that young Pinkerton announced as the robbers: Cole and Jim Younger, Frank and Jesse James, Jim Cummins, and Charlie Pitts.

Cole did as always when, on a rare occasion, he was not

guilty: he shouted to high heaven that he was not there; in fact, he wrote a letter that was published, telling the world that he was plumb innocent, that he had been in Louisiana at the time, and that his brothers had been in Dallas. Cole was very much hurt that anyone had suspected him of such a reprehensible bit of business. This was Cole's protective coloration. If he was innocent, he shouted at the top of his voice; if guilty, he was quiet. My own opinion, after studying the matter, is that Cole was not there. Anyway, the robbery, from the point of view of the riders, was a whopping success; they'd made a good haul and not a man had been nicked.

Now and then Cole let one of his brothers flop out of the nest and try his wings. Bob tried it September 26, 1872, with Frank and Jesse James flopping along beside him. Kansas City was having a county fair at the edge of town and everybody was having a wonderful time. Money had been coming into the box office all day from concessions and the selling of tickets. Arrangements had been made with the First National Bank of Kansas City to stay open late to receive the money, which was mostly bills. Suddenly three horsemen appeared at the cash office where the people bought their tickets. One of the horsemen covered the man inside the booth; another of the horsemen hopped off his horse and went inside the booth; the third rider held the two horses. The man who had gone inside snatched up the bills and dumped them into the grain sack. Then the three horsemen rode away with never a thank you.

The country boys, who were serving as police, were alerted, but they had no horses to pursue the evil men. In fact, no pursuit was organized; no posse rode determinedly after the three men. No one was arrested; not a soul suffered. The men scooped up $8,000. Bob had done quite well for a beginner. He'd got into an easy business.

The conflict between Cole and Jesse was growing. Matters suddenly became worse. Jesse also began to write letters to the newspapers. For years he had been a gray wolf, seen only at night in the timber; now he wrote boldly. He wrote a letter to the *Kansas City Times,* published August 16, 1876, which was as hot as a pistol barrel after a holdup. He said he hadn't been at the Otterville, Missouri, lawn party, as Hobbs Kerry had sworn in a court statement. Jesse was quite stirred up to have a lie told about himself, poor, misunderstood Jesse. By indirection Jesse said that Cole was there, while he himself was as innocent as Mary's lamb. He not only said he wasn't there but said that he could give the names of eight good men and true who would swear he wasn't. He also said that the papers charged that the James boys and the Youngers were at Russellville. Not true, he said. He said that he was at the Chaplin Hotel, Chaplin, Kentucky, and that he could prove this by fifty men. (Jesse was not a man to understate.) Frank, he said, had been hard at work on a ranch in San Luis Obispo County, California.

Cole was thoroughly and completely mad. There is no record of what he said to Jesse. It's a pity there isn't.

But the two were tied together whether they liked it or not.

Jesse was proud of his leadership. He ruled with an iron hand. But Cole Younger was challenging his authority. Cole had brought in two of his brothers and now the balance of power was falling to Cole. Jesse didn't like this and he meant to do something about it.

And he did. He went to Cole and said, "Cole, y'know George Shepherd don't like you and he's fixin' to kill you the first chance he gets."

Cole was stunned—one of his best friends going to kill him—a man he had ridden with under Quantrill and had been with at Lawrence. But these were hard days; no man knew whom to trust. Well, he wouldn't let George get the drop on him. He'd fill him fuller of lead than a bullet mold.

One night Cole stopped at the home of Silas Hudspeth, who lived near Six Mile Church, and hallooed.

Hudspeth appeared at the door. "Who is it?"

"A friend, Silas," said Cole, for one didn't shout his name into the night.

Hudspeth recognized the voice. "Come in."

Cole went in. A fire was started and the two began to visit.

It was not long until there was another shout and Hudspeth went to the door. "Who is it?"

"Hello, Silas! Can I come it?"

Cole was flabbergasted to see George Shepherd walk in. And when Shepherd saw Cole he could hardly believe his eyes. One sat on one side of the fireplace, the other on the other. But neither mentioned the feud between them.

The evening wore on. "Well, I guess it's time to turn in," said the hospitable Hudspeth. "I'm a bachelor, like you know, an' I got only two beds. I'm used to sleepin' in mine, so I reckon you two'll have to bunk together."

The two went into the bedroom and began taking off their boots, watching each other closely.

George Shepherd got into bed with his trousers on, put himself against the wall, and lay so he would face Cole. In his hand was a six-shooter.

Cole took off his boots and lay down on the outside of the bed, his pistol in his hand, facing Shepherd—the two certainly making the strangest bedmates that ever came together in the hospitable state of Missouri.

When one stirred, the other was instantly alert.

It was a long night.

At last it was over, and the two came into the kitchen the next morning where the host was cheerfully preparing breakfast. "How did you two sleep?"

"Fine," said George Shepherd.

"Like a log," said Cole, as he edged into a chair on the opposite side of the table from hollow-eyed Shepherd.

After breakfast, when the two went out to feed their horses, Shepherd said, "Cole, why do you want to kill me? We've always been friends. Now you're tryin' to get the drop on me."

"Because you want to kill me," said Cole.

"Why, Cole," said the astonished man, "I never had it in mind to kill you till Jess told me you was goin' to kill me, so naturally I had to protect myself."

"Why, George, Jess told me you wanted to kill me."

The two compared notes. It was a plot for one of them to kill the other, Jesse not caring which.

"I think we ought to shake hands an' be friends again," said Cole, reaching out a mighty paw.

"We sure can, Cole," said George Shepherd, and the two shook hands.

The incident shows something of the life that the wanted men were living. Who was whose friend? That was the question these riders of the night asked. Everybody's hand was against them. How long could they last?

CHAPTER VII

The Incident at Sainte Genevieve, Missouri, Where Everything Didn't Go Exactly Right

THERE IT WAS again: that old problem—where to find a fat goose. It would have to be a new town—one that had never been visited, for after a robbery a town armed itself as if expecting the Army of the Wilderness. At about this time The Boys heard of what might be rich plucking at Sainte Genevieve, in Swampeast Missouri, hard by the Mississippi River. The town was what was called quaint. It had been settled by the French and French people walked upon the streets; many were newcomers from faraway France, and many spoke with a French accent.

It was to this town on May 26, 1873, that Jesse and his friends rode, not attracted by the quaintness of the town but by the Sainte Genevieve Savings Association which had *beaucoup* francs. The men rode into town as they always did, from two different directions—this time, two from one direction, three from another, all converging in the center of the town.

The five travelers paused before the bank, not in order to admire its quaintness. Three of them got off their horses and walked briskly into the bank as if eager to do business with it. That was exactly the situation, as soon developed. One of the two remaining horsemen got off his horse and held the other horses. The fifth member of the visiting group drew a pistol from under his linen duster and sat with it in his hand, his eyes moving up and down the delightful old street.

When the three men entered the bank, the cashier looked up and smiled at the new customers. *"Bonjour, messieurs.* What is it I can do for you today?"

"You can hand us your money," said one of the callers.

The cashier smiled at the man's delightful humor.

"Certainement! But first you must put some in."

"Hand it over and be quick about it," said another of the rude callers, and shoved a pistol at the cashier.

"But no," said the cashier. "It is not that we should do so. I am sorry, *messieurs,* but it is not to be."

"I tell you to hand over the money," said an uncultured voice.

The two other callers had pistols in their hands and pointed them at the employees.

One of the callers displayed a grain sack. "Put the money in here," he said harshly.

The cashier gathered up some bills and dropped them in as if he had glue on his fingers.

"Faster. Hurry up," said one of the men and leaned over and jabbed the cashier with his pistol. The man then turned his pistol on the other employees who took the hint, and began tossing in the money as fast as if it burned their fingers.

At last all the money in sight was reposing in the dark depths of the grain sack. One of the callers then took the grain sack, went to the door, and left the banking institution. The two other men followed close upon his heels. Not a shot had been fired.

The five men mounted their horses and galloped down the street as fast as the horses would take them.

One of the horses stumbled and threw the rider *plop* upon the ground. The rider was the one who was carrying the bag with its precious contents. He clung to the bag and now, bag in hand, he tried to catch the horse. It soon developed that the horse did not want to be caught. The two for a moment played a cat-and-mouse game, the mouse, in this case, being the man. At last the man caught the horse, placed the bag on the horse's neck in front of the saddle, and started to mount. At this most unpropitious moment the fractious horse gave a leap and away went horse, bag, and all—all except the man who was left, looking as if the horse had fallen on him.

Just at this moment a Frenchman came riding up. The man on the ground pointed to the flying horse and said, "Catch him. He's running away"—a situation that the Frenchman, no doubt, could see for himself.

"*Oui, monsieur,*" said the Frenchman. "That I shall be delighted to do, but how much is it that I am to be paid?"

The man on foot stared in astonishment.

"Catch that horse," he shouted, and drew an evil-looking pistol.

"*Mais non!*" said the Frenchman, not realizing that he was dealing with a hardhearted man. "It is not that I have to pursue a horse that belongs to another."

The man on foot turned the pistol straight at the Frenchman. "Catch that horse or I'll kill you."

"*Vraiment!*" said the Frenchman, and dashed after the fleeing animal. Finally, after a bit of maneuvering, he caught the horse and brought him back to the bandit. "*Voilà!*" said the Frenchman, proud of his deed. "And now, monsieur, how much is it that you should pay for my small kindness?"

"Nothing! Get out of here," said the unappreciative man, and leaped into the saddle once more.

The Frenchman stared after the flying bandit, uttering, as he did so, words that would have shocked Louis XVI.

A posse was quickly organized, as was always done on such occasions. And it accomplished just what all posses did —nothing.

It was a big day for the riders from Clay, for when the money was counted up there was almost $4,000.

The five horsemen (according to Robertus Love) were Cole Younger, Bob Younger, Clell Miller, Jesse James, and Bill Chadwell. I am not sure that Cole was there, search the records as I have. One reason that makes me think he wasn't there was that no description of a large bland man was turned in. And there was Cole's way of doing when he was innocent. He proclaimed he was in St. Clair County, Missouri, taking care of an old guerrilla friend. And he gave his friend's name —Murphy—and the name of the doctor, Dr. L. Lewis. I am inclined to believe that Cole was telling the truth. If he'd been at Sainte Genevieve he wouldn't have made a peep. Cole was accused of many things he didn't do, but even with this, he was still ahead of the game.

CHAPTER VIII

Cole Visits Belle in Texas and Sees Their Daughter. Belle's First Robbery. Some Cuff Notes on Jim Reed

O NE IS APT to think of Cole as always on horseback, riding here and there across the country, but this is hardly true. To throw the officers off, he often appeared in strange disguises and at unexpected places. An example of this is told by Dolph Shaner in his book *The Story of Joplin*. The incident was related to him by Charlie Glover, the paymaster. The story is this:

Once Cole decided to go into the business of banditry for himself and persuaded two of his brothers to go in with him. The three were traveling through the Ozarks in a covered wagon on one of their officer-dodging trips from Texas to Missouri. A covered wagon was an excellent disguise; no one would ever think that "movers" would have an unworthy idea in their heads. The three came to Joplin and camped at about Fifteenth and St. Louis avenues. Their wagon was drawn by two exceedingly good horses, one horse being led behind. The men learned that the following day was to be payday for the lead miners at the Joplin Mining and Smelting Company.

They found that the money was to be handed out in a little wooden building on John Street, north of Broadway, near present Landreth Avenue. They surveyed the surroundings. One of them would hold the horses outside; two would go in, grab the pie, then away they would go, over hill and dale.

The two walked in—and got a shock. The paymaster was Charlie Glover, nephew of the Fletch Taylor who had been the spy for Quantrill in getting information for the sacking of Lawrence, Kansas. Cole knew him well, for they had fought side by side.

"Oh! Is that you, Charlie?" mumbled Cole. "This is quite a surprise. Well, how is Fletch Taylor? Is he all right?"

The paymaster went on handing out money. "Fletch is just fine, Cole. He'll be along any minute." The paymaster handed out some more gold pieces and some greenbacks. "Sit down and wait. I'll soon be through, and when Fletch comes we'll all go out and have supper together."

"That'll be fine," said Cole with the manner of a man who enjoys good food and stimulating conversation.

The five had supper together, and when the evening was over Cole and his brothers led their fine horses back to their shaky old covered wagon.

There is another instance of Cole disguising himself in an unusual way. Once, when he was being pressed by the law, he hid himself away in the Ozarks where he chanced to meet a traveling "eye doctor." Cole robbed the unlucky man and told him to get out of the country or he would kill him. Cole took the man's equipment, his box of assorted spectacles, and went to Caddo Gap, Arkansas, where he set up in business under the name of "Dr. Shrewsbury." He let the hill-billies try on the glasses until they found a pair that would "fit." In addition he told the people to bathe their eyes regularly in a weak solution of sassafras tea, a remedy he had learned from his mother. He remained two weeks, then left.

The hill people could not understand why their eye doctor should so suddenly leave without bidding them good-by.

James P. Holman, who lives in Richmond, Missouri, told me the following story about his great-uncle Fred Holman. The latter, as a boy of twelve, was riding along the road when he saw five horsemen approaching—none other than the dreaded James-Younger gang. They told the boy to consider himself their prisoner and to come with them. They camped that night in the woods and made him do some of the camp work but did not treat him unkindly. One thing that they did give him was an insight into how the outlaws lived. When they were being pursued and came to a crossroad, they continued along one road for some fifty yards, then turned off into the grass, and doubled back. When they came to a crossing, they proceeded along another road. And here the boy was made to take willow sprouts and brush away the tracks so they would not show. When the posse came, they saw the easily noted tracks and rode hotly after them, the robbers, meantime, going in another direction. The outlaws kept the boy about a week, then let him return home, unharmed; in fact, said my informant, the boy kind of enjoyed it.

An instance of the things that happened to the James-Younger outlaws was told to me by Harry C. Hoffman, who has already been identified. He said:

"In 1909 Frank James told me this story. Frank was known to his friends and the men in his band as Buck, which was his mother's pet name for him; in fact, she rarely called him anything else. One day Frank James, Arch Clements, and George Shepherd rode horseback into a small town in Texas, when they were on the scout. Arch Clements went into a saloon to imbibe some refreshment. Neither Frank nor George drank, so they went into a small hotel and sat down in the lobby to get a change of scene. They got it, all right, for about this time the town marshal came in and recognized them. Pretending not to know them, he went out and got his deputy and came back. Suddenly the two whipped out their pistols and shouted, 'Hands up! You're under arrest.' Frank James leaped to his feet and began shooting—wildly, it's true, but shooting. George Shepherd, in trying to leap to his feet, got a foot tangled up in the rungs of a chair and fell sprawling on the floor where he kept shouting, 'Give 'em hell, Buck! Give 'em hell!' Buck did give 'em hell, and the two managed to get to their horses. They shouted to Arch Clements, and the three hit for the brush as fast as they could travel. Frank James often reminded George Shepherd of the incident, who had to admit it was true. 'Give 'em hell, Buck,' became a kind of byword among the gang, and later, when the survivors met at reunions, they used it laughingly."

Cole went once or twice to see Belle and the child, but there was always a row with her father. And there were the pleadings and heartbroken sobs of her mother, and Preston Shirley's downright hatred of him. He decided to brave all this and go, anyway, for he still felt affection for Belle. And this he did in the fall of 1872. The closer he got to Scyene, the more eager he was to see Belle and Pearl. Belle, as he knew, had a hot temper, but she also had a warm heart and she was "good company." No one was ever bored in her presence.

At last the long ride was over and he was in Texas and on the way to John Shirley's house—the very house where he had met Belle the day that now seemed so long ago. Shirley was in the yard chopping firewood.

"Hello, Mr. Shirley," called Cole warmly.

Shirley looked up in surprise, his ax in his hand. "What do you want?"

"I want to see Belle and the baby and all of you," said Cole, rebuffed by Shirley's cold manner.

"What do you want to see them about?"

"I've come all the way to see them," said Cole, ill at ease. "Is there anything the matter?"

Shirley split another block of wood with spiteful blows. "There's plenty the matter."

"What's wrong?" asked the mystified Cole.

"I'll call her an' you can find out for yourself. It'd been better if you hadn't come. Myra!"

In a moment Belle appeared in the door. "Cole," she managed to say.

"I guess I kind of took you by surprise."

"Tell him to go, Myra," said John Shirley. "He won't help matters none. It was a sad day for you the day he pulled up here the first time."

Cole looked from one to the other, puzzled.

Belle stood looking at Cole, then away from him. "Cole," she choked, "I'm married."

"Married?" repeated Cole.

"You didn't come back, and people were talking an' saying things about little Pearl. I had to do something."

"Who are you married to, Belle?"

"To Jim Reed."

"I guess I ought to know him," said Cole bitterly. "He rode with me durin' war days."

"I used to know him in Missouri, Rich Hill. One day he rode in here—just like you did. He had some friends with him, like you had. He asked me to marry him, and I did. We were married on horseback."

"On horseback?"

"John Fisher performed the wedding; he pronounced us man and wife."

"It was a mock wedding," said John Shirley bitterly. "He wasn't no more a preacher'n I am. But it was a better wedding than yours," he said, looking at Cole belligerently.

The three talked for some time, Cole asking questions and trying to get a grasp of all that had happened. "Where's little Pearl?" he asked finally.

"Taking a nap. I'll get her up. You and Pa talk till I get her ready."

"I've said all I've got to say," declared Shirley. He picked up the ax, and began to chop; each time he swung the ax he gave a little grunt. "Is there money on your head?"

"Yes," said Cole.

"How much?"

"A thousand dollars."

Shirley began to chop again.

"I haven't been in a lot of things they've accused me of," said Cole.

"Uh-huh!" said Shirley as he swung the ax. "Are you still with Jess and Frank?"

"I see them occasionally."

"Is money on their heads?"

"Yes."

"Ever since you rode up here that time this place has been overrun with outlaws, an' I don't like it."

Belle came to the door. "Come in, Cole."

He could hardly believe his eyes when he saw how much Pearl had grown. Why, she was three now! Cole held out his arms encouragingly.

"Go on, Pearl," urged Belle.

The child would not advance; instead, she edged even farther away from him.

"Jim Reed says she is the prettiest child he ever saw."

"Where is Jim?" asked Cole, stirred with sudden jealousy.

"He's away, riding. He comes and goes," she added vaguely.

Cole took out his watch and displayed it temptingly. The child stared blankly.

"She's still about half asleep. She's a good child," Belle added. "I don't know what I'd do without her, Pa's so contrary."

"She's pretty."

Belle nodded. "Everybody says that. What are you doing now, Cole?"

"About the same thing. I want to buy a farm an' settle down. I was goin' to talk the idea over with you."

"It's too late now."

"I know it is. I just mention it because so many things come to my mind."

Instead of looking at each other, the two made a fuss over the child.

"Have you told her about me?" asked Cole.

"No. I didn't think I ought."

There was a painful silence. Cole stood up. "I'll have to go, Belle." He again held out his arms to the child, but she backed away. "Well, good-by, Belle. I wish you the best of luck. You're in my mind all the time."

"Good-by, Cole. I wish you hadn't stayed away so long...."

He looked at her tenderly. "Here's something to remember me by." He gave her a pistol.

He went outside. Shirley rested the head of his ax on the ground.

"I'm goin' now, Mr. Shirley."

"I see you are," said Shirley, and resumed his chopping.

Cole went to Dallas, where he remained three days gambling and "seeing the sights." But he didn't drink. Then he got on his horse and started on the long ride back to Missouri.

It had been an emotional moment for Belle when Cole had ridden away and left her. Her horseback marriage to Reed had been a mock one, but she was accepted as his wife and would have to remain so.

The contrast between the two men was sharp. Cole was well educated for the time, was genial and likable. Reed was a tall, hawk-faced, sandy-haired, mean-natured man, scant on education.

I was unable to find anything authoritative about Jim Reed; available only were the rewrites of the *Police Gazette* fabrications, so I wrote to Leon W. Mathews, editor of the *Bates County Republican*, Rich Hill, Missouri. This is his letter:

I love to run errands for Missouri writers, so yesterday I drove out into the country near Bethel Church, where there is still a big bunch of Reeds. I found his first cousin William M. Reed and had a big talk with him. He is eighty-seven and as Jim Reed was killed eighty-one years ago, this Reed has only family stories to tell. This is what I learned from him:

Jim Reed was born eight miles from Rich Hill where his father had quite a chunk of land. Jim himself was a rough character and was quite a man with his fists and liked to fight. The family moved to Carthage where the Shirley family ran an inn, and there Jim met Belle Starr, as she came to be known, aged thirteen, Jim being aged seventeen. Belle's father did not like Jim and this feeling developed into an open quarrel which ended up in a shooting match. No blood. Jim gravitated into outlawry and rode with the James-Youngers. Jim was a tough character.

Mrs. Gertrude Higgins wrote me from the Tate Nursing Home, Neosho, Missouri:

"When I was a young girl I went to the same church with Belle Starr, which was the Bethel Baptist Church, near Reed's Creek, near Rich Hill. Belle and her daughter both came to church horseback, riding sidesaddle. Her daughter went by the name of Pearl Starr. The thing that impressed me most was how devoted Belle was to her daughter and what fine clothes she had for her. Even during the sermon, Belle would look at the daughter instead of the preacher."

The Reeds were Southern sympathizers but their sympathies were not strong enough to make them want to take part in the war. To escape war, the family moved to Carthage as fast as wagons would take them. In spite of their flight, the war caught up with Jim Reed and he began to ride as a guerrilla.

After the war, Reed got into a neighborhood feud and killed two men. He headed for Texas. Soon there was a reward on his head of $1,000. Reed heard there was a nest of Missourians near Scyene and there he went. To his delight he found Belle. She was low in spirits, having, seemingly, lost Cole, and so she listened to his pleasant words and Carthage memories. It was not long until the horseback marriage was performed and now, to all intents and purposes, the two were man and wife, an unlucky stroke for her.

Things got so hot for Reed that he had to move again—this time to California with Belle and Pearl. Here a child was born and was named Ed Reed. And so now Belle had two children: Pearl Younger and the boy.

Just how Jim Reed made a living in California was not known. He was accused of two robberies, the low number being, no doubt, a charitable view. Anyway, he returned to

Texas and bought a farm near his father-in-law's; how he
got the money is not a matter of public record.

A kind of desperation came over Belle. Reed talked of
robbery matter-of-factly. And so what at first had seemed
shocking she began to accept as a way of life.

On the North Canadian River in the Indian Territory,
lived a minor chief of the Creeks. The government was giving the Indians subsidies and he was a kind of banker for his
fellow tribesmen. His name was Watt Grayson. One day
four robbers rode up to his lonely cabin; one was smaller
than the other three—Belle in men's clothes. One of the
robbers was Dan Evans who, later, was hanged by Judge
Parker, as told in my book *He Hanged Them High*. The
Indian would not disclose where the money was hidden. The
robbers cruelly tortured him and finally got the information
and $30,000. Then they rode away. The date was November
30, 1873.

What had happened to Belle since she had married Jim
Reed? In school she had been a bright, attractive girl whose
worst failing was a hasty temper. Now she was taking part in
a torture robbery. What strange metamorphosis had come
over her? Was it an echo of the times? Was she, too, a
victim of the border warfare and, later, the Civil War? Was
it losing, or seeming to lose, Cole? Or was it Reed's wily
ways?

Shortly after the robbery Belle went to Dallas where she
lived at the Planters' House and where she had plenty of
money. Jim Reed himself wasn't allowed to live so elegantly, for the law was hard upon him and he had to "go on
the scout."

Not too long after this, April 7, 1874, to be exact, the
stagecoach running between San Antonio and Austin experienced a bit of unpleasantness. As it was approaching the town

of Blanco, Texas, three men—one noticeably shorter than the others—stepped out in front. The three turned their attention to the passengers. Out came the grain sack, as of yore, and to this the passengers were invited to contribute. Then the mailbags were split open and whatever seemed likely was dumped into the grain sack. Finally the horses were cut loose and sent flying down the road. And soon the robbers were flying down the road, too, richer by $2,500, plus what the mailbags had surrendered.

There was a tremendous hue and cry in Texas. The governor of that great state offered a reward of $3,000; the United States mail agent offered the same amount, and the stage line offered $1,000—in all quite a sizable sum.

It was not long before the law wanted to talk to Jim Reed, but Jim was not available. The hills had him. One of the men on his trail was Deputy Sheriff John T. Morris who in three months wormed himself into Reed's confidence. This is the way William M. Reed, the cousin just mentioned, tells what happened:

"Down in Texas, about 1874, Jim and a man named John T. Morris, who was a deputy sheriff, were riding along the road, horseback. There was a reward on Jim's head and Morris wasn't unmindful of the situation. They came to a farmhouse and decided to go in and get the woman to cook up something. Morris said that sight of their guns would make the woman nervous and suggested they leave them on their saddles, which was done. After the two had eaten, Morris said he had swallowed a fly and would have to go out and relieve himself. He hurried to the horses, retrieved his pistol, slipped it into his pocket, and came back where Jim was sitting. Suddenly he whipped out his six-shooter and said, 'Jim, I'm arresting you on the charge of robbery. Now don't make me any trouble.' Jim leaped up, seized the table, and rushed upon Morris. Morris seized the table and the two wrestled all over the room, grunting and cursing, the lady of the house screaming, making, in all, quite a fracas. Jim began pummelin' Morris in the face with his fist. Morris shot through the table and hit Jim in the stomach. In a few minutes Jim was dead. Morris's face was pulpy, for Jim had given him some lusty blows. I don't know whether Morris got the money or not, but I know he got a good beating up."

The rest of the story is from the *Dallas Daily Herald* for August 28, 1874, the *Austin Weekly Democratic Statesman* for August 9, 1874, and from the *Galveston Daily News* for Sunday, August 9, 1874. The date of the shooting was August 6, 1874. The story put together from these papers is as follows:

Morris put the body into the farmer's spring wagon and started with it to Paris, a distance of fifteen miles. The day was hot—August in Texas. When the body got to the town it was unwrapped; many looked at it as it lay in the spring wagon and identified it. There was no one to claim the body, so it was consigned to the potter's field. A driver was engaged, but by this time the body was so decomposed that the driver became sick and lost his way. He dumped the body out of the spring wagon, left it beside the road, drove back to town, and notified the sheriff. The sheriff took the body and interred it in the potter's field. Belle was at her father's at Scyene and did not see the body and had nothing to do with its burial.

(*Note:* The *Police Gazette* legend that Belle refused to identify the body to keep Morris from getting the reward is not true. Belle never saw the body.)

And now, at the age of twenty-six, Belle was free. Would

Cole come back? she asked herself. And how would her beloved Pearl get along? Pearl was now five.

Reed was killed the first week in August, but the news did not get to Cole until November, for Belle was not yet famous and news about her was not of national interest. What Cole had been hoping for had now happened: Belle was free. He would slip down to Texas to see her. But slipping down to Texas was not as easy as it had once been, for there was the reward on his head; a thousand sheriffs and deputy sheriffs, as well as a squad of Pinkertons, were aching to see him. Cole knew they would be watching his old haunts, and so he waited. As soon as he could he would go to see Belle.

CHAPTER IX

The James-Youngers Rob Their First Train. The Year 1874 Is a Wonderfully Prosperous One for "The Boys"

THE BANKS were more and more on the alert; it was harder and harder to swoop down on them. And then Jesse and his stalwarts decided to have a go at something that was comparatively new in the hit-and-run business—railroad robbery. The first train robbery had taken place May 5, 1865, hard upon the close of the Civil War. An Ohio & Mississippi train running from St. Louis to Cincinnati was derailed by ruffians near North Bend, Ohio. The men helped themselves to the contents of the express car, robbed the passengers, scooted across the river in skiffs, and disappeared from history. The men were ex-guerrillas, not real train robbers, but they initiated armed train robbery.

The art was really invented by the Reno brothers, near Seymour, Indiana, October 6, 1866, the same year in which the Liberty bank had been breached. The Reno brothers had done exceedingly well and had picked $13,000—a haul that any robber could be proud of. But there was a catch. The law got them, and their leader, John Reno, was soon busy making binder twine. And his three brothers were dead from rope strangulation, not properly and sedately dead, but crudely at the hands of an angry mob. The professional career of the Reno brothers lasted a scant two years. It just goes to show the difference between Missouri and Indiana. The Hoosier boys never did get the knack.

Jesse and Cole, the two leaders, thought it over. They would do some train robbing themselves. Everything was in their favor (or so they thought). They were experienced men. They were fearless. They knew how to get away from irate posses.

But which railroad? They would have to move to a state where people were not suspicious and where the Pinkertons were not snooping around. They heard that the Chicago, Rock Island & Pacific Railway was regularly engaged in sending shipments of gold from the glowing West to Chicago. Gold!

They were men of action. They rode immediately and forthwith to Iowa to try their hand. In some way that is not known they got word that an unusually large shipment of gold was on its way to Chicago on the night of July 21, 1873. They went to the quiet little town of Adair, Iowa, which had never seen anything more exciting than a taffy pull, and there started their preparations. Adair was a few miles east of Council Bluffs, on the way to Chicago. The men rode by twos and arrived about nine o'clock at night. The town, as usual, was softly slumbering. Not a mouse was stirring. Not even the town watchman.

The men went out a short distance, broke into a handcar shed, took a spike bar and hammer, pried off a fishplate, and pulled out the spikes. Then they tied a rope to the rail in such a manner that the rail could be pulled out of alignment. When everything was taken care of, the men hid behind an embankment on a curve where the train would have to slow up.

At about midnight the train came in sight.

The rope was pulled.

The men had thought that the train would stop when its wheels rolled off the rails, but instead the train toppled over on its side, killing the engineer. Women and children screamed in a truly heartrending scene.

But not all was tragedy. In the daycoach were thirty Chinese. Their passage money had been paid by a church organization that wanted to take them out of heathen China and show them how a Christian country lived. Some of the Chinese could speak a little English which they had learned in the church schools in China.

Suddenly the dozing Chinese were flung violently about. They screamed at the top of their voices and came tumbling out of the coach. The bandits, wanting to quiet the overseas visitors, fired into the air. The Chinese screamed louder than ever. The bandits stood, baffled; never had they had to face such a situation. Finally they herded the Chinese back into the car. The Chinese did not seem to know they were learning Christian ways.

The robbers, almost defeated by the lowly Chinese, went to the express car and forced the guard to open the safe—no pickax needed. But all they got was $3,000, a trifling sum for the heretofore successful men. The next night, at exactly the same hour, $75,000 came rolling through. The robbers missed the Big Haul by twenty-four hours.

The bandits, angered by the small amount of money that the express car yielded, went down the aisle of the passenger cars with the familiar grain sack. Then they went to the coach where the Chinese were, opened the sack, and told the Chinese to contribute. The Chinese, knowing nothing about American ways, looked into the grain sack to see what was there. One of the bandits made signs of emptying his pockets, so that the Chinese would know what to do. But the Chinese didn't have pockets, so they again looked into the mysterious bag. Finally the bandits started out, uttering words that the Chinese had never heard in their church schools. Taking the thin grain sack with them, the bandits mounted their horses and rode away.

Since it would be hours before the train could be righted, the crew decided to walk the passengers to the nearest town, which was Anita, Iowa. After a great deal of shouting, the train crew got the passengers started down the railroad track, following a brakeman with a lantern. The next thing was to get the Chinese to do likewise. They wore soft-soled slippers and did not want to pad down a railroad track after a man with a lantern. The train crew had to shout to make the Chinese understand. At last the Chinese started, saying things that, fortunately, the train crew did not understand. Finally the pilgrims reached the little town where the train crew ordered food for the passengers and where the spirits of the bedraggled people revived.

Back at the wreck, an emergency telegraph was set up and cut into the main line. Word flashed that the train had been wrecked and robbed. A wrecking train was soon on its way.

The train crew then pounded on the doors of the sleepy farmers and told them of the terrible thing that had happened and asked the farmers to chase the bandits. The farmers said they hadn't lost any money and the railroad could chase its own robbers. The railroad then dispatched word to its agents in that section to organize posses among the townspeople. A special posse train pulled out of Council Bluffs with enough men to take Sitting Bull. Nothing came of it.

Meantime the rich state of Iowa stepped into the case and offered the meager reward of $600. The railroad, disappointed by the small sum the state offered, said it would pay

$5,000 to anyone who would apprehend one of the robbers. There were no takers.

Finally, at the scene of the robbery, after much urging, sixty men with rusty fowling pieces got on fat farm horses and gently chased the outlaws. They didn't get near enough to the Missourians to fire a shot, possibly a good thing for them.

As far as the James-Youngers were concerned, the robbery was a success; it is true they got only a small sum, but there were no arrests and the men got safely back to the haven of Missouri.

(NOTE: Ah me! Time works changes. Instead of being mad as hornets, the people of Adair are now proud of what happened that night long ago. On the eightieth anniversary the town had a "Jesse James Day." The Rock Island Railroad sent a train of that period, with a dining car, and re-enacted the scene with four television camera crews grinding like mad. Not only this, but the people of the town and the management of the railroad put up a plaque to honor the event. It reads: "Site of the first train robbery in the West. Committed by the notorious Jesse James and his gang of outlaws, July 21, 1873." So wags the world.)

Business was booming. Eighteen seventy-four was a fine year.

January 15—The Boys had good success in Hot Springs, Arkansas. Not a man was lost.

January 31—Things went fine at Gad's Hill, Missouri.

March 10—They knocked off a Pinkerton man: Detective John W. Witcher.

(A bit of awkwardness arose over the killing of Detective Witcher. Jesse killed him, but carted the body across the Missouri River from Clay County and dropped it in Cole's county so that Cole would be suspected. When Cole learned about this he was as mad as a wet hen. He didn't want to be accused of murders he didn't commit.)

March 16—Killed two more Pinkerton snoopers near Osceola, Missouri.

April 7—The San Antonio stage robbery was a clean, satisfactory job. Not a man was lost.

April 24—Jesse got himself married. Not a minute was lost.

December 13—A successful train robbery at Muncie, Kansas. Things couldn't have gone better.

The next year, however, things didn't go so well. But, as all businessmen know, that is to be expected. Some years up, some down. In fact, in 1875 The Boys added only one feather to their bonnet. On September 1 they paid a courtesy call on the bank in Huntington, West Virginia, and picked up $2,000. It was discouraging. But you can't strike twelve every time.

In 1875 something happened that caused Cole no end of trouble. The James-Youngers were known from coast to coast—the most ferocious outlaw group in America. "Dime novels" battened on them, falling from the presses like apples from a shaken tree. Jesse and Frank rated first in villainy, with Cole close upon their heels. Augustus C. Appler, a man from Maryland who had lived briefly in Osceola, Missouri, wrote a book entitled *The Guerrillas of the West; or the Life, Character and Daring Exploits of the Younger Brothers*. The cover title was *Younger Brothers*. It was published in St. Louis by "John T. Appler, publisher and proprietor." The following year it was reprinted by the Eureka Publishing Company, St. Louis. The book was printed and reprinted until 1892; the latter copyright was by Laird & Lee, Chicago. The book was sold on endless trains where the people shook every time the train stopped. The story the book told was up to 1875, while The Boys were still kicking. After the Northfield bank robbery, a new edition was hastily scrambled together and the story of the robbery included. And there the book ended. There is no evidence that Appler ever saw Cole; never does he quote him. The book is mostly an account of the border battles that Cole or other guerrillas took part in. These accounts are good and they are accurate. But when Appler moves over into the realm of outlawry, he tells little or nothing. Most of what he does set down is to prove, when a robbery was committed, that Cole was far, far away, doing kind deeds to the deserving which was the attitude at this time of many people in Missouri; and this attitude Appler passed along. The book is a reservoir of information about almost everything except Cole and his days as an outlaw. In fact, Appler doesn't mention the last forty-one years of Cole's life.

I tell all this because there was something in the book that in later years caused Cole trouble; in fact, Cole came to hate Appler bitterly. On page 76 is the "Prisoner Story," the most crushing editorial avalanche that ever fell on Cole:

Upon one occasion Quantrill's band encountered a party of Jayhawkers, numbering thirty or more. A dozen of the Jayhawkers were killed and fifteen captured. They were taken to camp where the question of their fate was soon decided. After supper, and while the shades of evening were approaching, Cole Younger got out his Enfield rifle captured that day. It was the finest he had ever seen, and its merits and demerits were discussed by the men. Opinions differed as to its superior qualities. One of the men remarked that he had heard it would kill at the distance of a mile. Younger replied, "If that is so, the force of the discharge must be terrific." Another banteringly remarked, "If the gun will kill at a mile, a ball, at a short range, would go through ten men." Younger raised up from his saddle upon which he had been sitting, and remarked, "It is easy to demonstrate." The fifteen prisoners were placed in a line, one behind the other. Cole Younger took the gun, played with the lock a moment to "get the hang of it," and then measured off fifteen paces in front of the line, wheeled about, looked carefully and soberly into the faces of the doomed men, and fired. The first, second, and third men dropped lifeless, without a groan. Muttering a contemptuous condemnation of the new rifle, Younger, without moving from his tracks, continued his experiments. Seven times the rifle was discharged, each time the guerrillas commenting carelessly upon the merits of the Enfield, until fifteen of the Jayhawkers lay in an inanimate heap upon the grass.

This story became important in the life and death of Cole Younger.

(PERSONAL COMMENT: One of my favorite dislikes in this book of Appler's is the Plank Fence story. In January 1863 Cole was about to be captured, but escaped by dashing out the back door of the house in his stocking feet. To keep his footprints from showing in the snow he got on top of a plank fence, walked half a mile—evidently on the edges of the planks—then leaped from the fence into the road. He made the mighty jump so that his footprints would be lost among the hoofmarks left by some cattle that providentially had passed along the road a bit earlier—a feat I have to this day never seen accomplished. But, for that matter, I have never seen a man in his stocking feet walk half a mile on the edges of a plank fence. And yet I was born and brought up not far from where this happened.)

Another sample of the Appler book's impossible stories:

One night Cole Younger went to the home of his grandmother, Mrs. Fristoe, where he stayed for supper, hitching his horse back of the house, in the brush. After eating supper and talking to the old lady for some time, Cole concluded he would return to camp. He bid the old lady good-bye, and walked out on the porch which was elevated some four feet from the ground and open underneath. The moon was shining brightly at the time. Just as he was about to step off the porch, he was surprised to meet his cousin Captain Charles Younger, of the State Militia (Federal). Both recognized each other and shook hands. After shaking hands, Captain Charles Younger said, "You are my prisoner." Cole scanned him closely for a moment and then, quick as lightning, grabbed his revolver, threw it into his face and fired, Captain Charles Younger dropping dead. Cole sprang from the porch and ran through the yard, as he discovered that the house was surrounded by Union soldiers. When near the fence and brush where his horse was, Cole fell over a bee-gum and dislocated his knee; at this very instant a shower of lead passed over him, cutting the back of his coat into ribbons, but not drawing blood. Had he not fallen the very instant he did, he would have been instantly killed. With his knee badly injured, Cole crawled to the brush, got on his horse, and made his escape.

This is the end of the amazing story. Its author neglected to tell how bullets could cut Cole's coat to ribbons without drawing blood, or how he could crawl with a dislocated knee, mount his horse, and escape with the enemy as thick as bees. Today if an author turned in such a wild story, he would have his shirt cut to ribbons by his editor, with, possibly, a few drops of blood.

It should also be pointed out that Cole had no cousin in the Union Army and that the story from beginning to end is a complete fabrication. But so were endless stories about Cole. Later these stories played hob with him.

Business continued good. The Boys were flushed with success. They were the finest bandits who ever roamed the range. They looked around to pick up some more loose change and decided they'd help themselves to the express car at Otterville, a town near Sedalia, Missouri. The date: July 7, 1876.

Practice makes perfect, they said, and so The Boys congregated at Otterville and piled wooden railroad ties across the track and set them on fire. In addition they had a young boy named Asbury Good-Knight to hold up a lantern. (He told me about it himself.)

The train came to a stop, and The Boys went to the express car, but all was not bright, all was not right. In fact, things were in the deuce of a shape. They found that the money had been put in a "through" safe; this meant that the safe had been locked when the train had left, and could not be opened till it got to Chicago and the duplicate key applied. It was maddening.

Jesse and his assistants gazed at the safe and the safe gazed defiantly back. It had the money and it proposed not to disgorge it. The safe, however, was of sheet iron and not wholly invulnerable. A fireman's hammer, used to break coal, was brought, and one of the men assaulted the surly safe. The safe quivered but gave not an inch.

"You see what you can do, Cole," said Jesse.

Cole, the biggest man in the group, looked around, and he found a sharp-pointed pick to be used in case of wreck attached to the wall. Then he found a piece of chalk used to mark information on a wooden bulletin board. He drew a circle on top of the safe, raised the pick aloft, and gave the safe a staggering blow. The safe budged not. Raising his pick again, he gave the safe a blast that made it tremble. But it still held fast to its trust. Growing indignant, Cole rained blows upon the doughty little safe. Finally there was an opening in the top, like a hole in a pirate's trunk. Now they could see the money. Cole tried to thrust in his massive hand, but the hole was too small and the money reposed undisturbed.

"I'll try," said Jesse. He had a small hand. He thrust his hand into the aperture.

Luck was his lady and he began to pull out greenbacks and silver. The thirsty grain sack was held up and it swallowed $14,000.

Then the hard-working men went to the passenger coach and walked down the aisle, holding out enticingly, as they did so, the grain sack, inviting all to toss in their money, wallets, and jewelry. And the passengers, looking at the guns, did as was suggested, complaining not at all.

When they went outside, the men fired a few shots into the air to keep anyone from peeping. Then they mounted their horses and rode off. The men escaped, one and all. Luck was still their companion. But more posses than ever were out on their trail; and more people than ever were aroused against them. And the matter wasn't completely and wholly a triumph, for later one of their men was arrested and sent to the penitentiary for four years to think it over. But the arrest was not made by the Pinkertons; the arrest was made by the St. Louis Police Department. The man who was tucked away in prison was Hobbs Kerry, whom no one ever accused of being an intellectual. He didn't know Shakespeare from Sylvanus J. Cobb, Jr. His job at the robbery was to hold the horses, a position he was eminently fitted for.

Meantime it was becoming more and more hazardous to take over a bank. The old way of asking for change for a $100 bill would no longer do. Every bank was alert and every person on the street was suspicious of any unusual activity in a bank. And the troublesome Pinkertons were buzzing about; it was true they hadn't yet stung a member of the present band, but one had to keep fanning his hat at them. One of their "operatives" said he had tracked his man to Clay County, Missouri, where he had disappeared. This was true, but something else was also true. The Pinkertons had lost three men and they didn't trust any person in Clay County; the people, said the Pinkertons, were all friends of the outlaws. And there was a great deal of truth in this. If not friends, they at least didn't want to court the enmity of the James-Youngers; in fact, no one in his right mind would. Cole was not so completely bent upon revenge. Jesse was the terrible one. If he felt that anyone was threatening his well-being—*ping!* and the matter was over.

They would have to move farther away from their seat of operations. But where? Bill Chadwell, a new student of banking, came forth with an idea. Minnesota! No one in Minnesota knew them. None of its banks had ever been robbed. The state was rich and the banks were as stuffed as bed ticks. Jesse was mistrustful of the idea. And so was Cole. He had grown disgusted with outlawry and wanted to get out of it. He decided he would make one more "ride," then return to Belle and Pearl in Texas.

But the others thought well of the idea. How would they get there? They couldn't ride horseback all that distance. They would go by train and buy their horses in Minnesota. There was plenty of money for that. The situation looked just mighty good.

CHAPTER X

The Greatest Band of Outlaws America Has Ever Known Arrives in Minnesota to Look into Banking Conditions

Elaborate plans were made, for this was to be the biggest haul. James Henry Younger was living quietly in California. He had been born on Cole's birthday and was four years younger than Cole. A letter arrived telling Jim to come back and join. He had given up outlawry and did not want to return, but group pressure was strong. He decided he would make one more ride. He was a quiet, well-mannered man, more of a "listener" than a talker.

Bob Younger was the baby of the expedition, twenty-three years old, a soft-spoken, rather likable lad. No one, meeting him as a stranger, would have guessed he was an outlaw.

The smartest was Cole. He had, in war and wickedness, killed sixteen men. The most dangerous man was Jesse. But in this summary Frank James must be reckoned with, as we shall soon see. He was the oldest—a year and five days older than Cole.

Clell Miller was the clown, a short, stocky boy with a hearty laugh, about the last man you would write down as an outlaw. Everybody liked him. He had been born near the James homestead and took great pride in being noticed by Jesse and Frank. Sometimes he stayed in the house when The Boys were there, a great event for him. He was their hero worshiper. His full name was Clelland Miller, no "Mc." His grandfather was Moses Miller, a blacksmith near Kearney and well known to Frank and Jesse. (The grandfather lies buried on the old family farm in what is known as Muddy Fork Cemetery. After the disaster at Northfield, Clell's body was brought back and buried beside his grandfather's, and there you can see the stone today with the name spelled Clelland.) When he found that The Boys were going to "ride North," he begged to go along. And because Jesse and Frank liked him, he was told that he could go. He was thrilled. He would ride with the famous James-Youngers!

Jesse James was the moodiest. When things were going well, he was genial and easy to get along with, but when things were going badly, he was cruel, demanding, and dangerous. He would stop at nothing. But also he was a natural leader, the one who planned and, when the time came, he was completely reckless. The man had no fear. He had a little baby nose, turned up.

In contrast to Jesse was Frank James, tall and thin, with a sharp aquiline nose and a high voice. He was the best-educated member of the band. Sometimes he rode with a copy of Shakespeare in his pocket; sometimes, as they jogged along, he would suddenly quote Shakespeare. It made the others blink.

Charlie Pitts looked more like an outlaw than any in the group. He lacked half an inch of being six feet, had a mass of thick black hair, wore a heavy mustache, and had a small goatee. In addition, he was dark-complexioned. And usually there was a scowl on his face. He had a rough way of talking; when he was aroused, this was almost a bark. He was given to swearing and cursing—this in contrast to Cole, who never swore.

In contrast to sinister Charlie Pitts was Bill Chadwell, a small man who seemed to have too many teeth. He was the "talker" of the group. Nothing was too trivial for him to comment on. On the other hand, Pitts was silent, only now and then putting in a word over Chadwell's chatter. And so they ranged up and down the human scale in age and temperament.

Full of confidence, the eight arrived in St. Paul. For a long time Luck had been their handmaiden; she would always smile on them. They would take care of the bank Bill Chadwell had suggested, then ride back to Missouri and disappear into thin air. The laugh would again be on the Pinkertons.

There was a great deal to be said for their self-confidence, for never in America had such a daring, reckless, capable band been assembled. Not a Hobbs Kerry among them. There was not one weak mind to hold the horses.

They separated and went to two hotels: the Merchants' Hotel and the European Hotel. In high spirits they attended a baseball game between the St. Paul Red Caps and the Winona Clippers on the last day of August 1876—the year of the Battle of the Little Big Horn. Soon, too, these men were to make their last stand.

Then they went to a gambling house on East Third Street, between Jackson and Robert streets, about half a block from the Merchants' Hotel, and had their fling. Cole won $300. Chadwell helped himself to about the same amount. Things were going fine.

They began to buy their horses. Jesse, Frank, Jim, and Clell Miller each got a horse in Red Wing. Bob and Chadwell each bought a horse in Mankato. Charlie Pitts and Cole each bought a horse in St. Peter. Cole paid $135 for his. The horses they bought were good ones. They would soon need just that kind.

In St. Peter, Cole and Charlie Pitts were sitting on the hotel porch, smoking cigars, when some boys came up and stood staring at the visitors, boylike. Cole reached into his pocket, and brought out a coin. "It belongs to the one who gets it," he said, tossing it among them. The boys scrambled for it. This was so much fun that Charlie Pitts fished out a coin and tossed it. The two continued to do this until they ran out of coins, laughing pleasantly at the boys. It was nice to be a rich gentleman.

Two matters must now be attended to: the horses must be broken not to shy at pistol shots; the men must learn the country. And this the men started to do. They posed as farm buyers and rode up and down the highways and byways, now and then popping off their pistols as they looked for farms to buy. They stopped farmers on the road, they even visited them in their homes and dickered. Cole and his men said they would pay cash; this was music to the farmers' ears.

Cole and Charlie Pitts went to the town of Madelia and registered at the Flanders House. With a flourish Cole signed himself "J. C. King." King was the name of a congressman from that district, and to Cole it seemed funny to use the name. Charlie Pitts signed himself "Jack Ladd." The latter had been a detective who had helped blow off Mrs. Samuel's arm. This, to rough and rowdy Charlie Pitts, was captivating humor.

The proprietor of the hotel, Thomas L. Vought, welcomed the two land-hungry men and tipped them off to the best farms in the section. They would pay cash, Cole explained, and they wouldn't haggle over a dollar or so an acre. The important thing was to get good, productive farms. Then Cole asked about the roads, rivers, and bridges. Cole said he did not want to get saddled with a farm where he couldn't get his products to market. The hotel man helped him with this top problem.

The eight land buyers rode up and down the countryside, but they didn't ride together. They rode by twos; when they were on lonely roads they accustomed their horses to pistol fire. And now, as the men got used to their horses, they found that they had bought good ones, and well they might, for horses were their line.

The big day came; they would make a professional call on the First National Bank, Mankato. At high noon the eight horsemen of Missouri rode by twos and threes from different directions and converged on the unsuspecting bank. But when they got there they found something that shocked their sensitive souls: a crowd was standing outside the bank. The Missouri men thought the word had got out that the bank was to be entered and that the people had come to see the fun. Never in all their riding experience had the men had to face such a situation. It was maddening. As a matter of fact, the people were watching repairs being made on a building across the street and paid no attention to the men. Jesse gave a sign and he and his men rode away, again by twos and threes. Jesse went from one group to another and told them that they would try again at two o'clock. And this they did. Another crowd had gathered and was solemnly staring at the repairs, after the immemorial way of busy people. Again Jesse made a sign and all rode away, pretty well disgusted with Minnesota banking methods.

They gathered outside of town. It would hardly do for eight horsemen to ride three times to the same place. Helpful Bill Chadwell thought up an idea: they would go to Northfield, which was about forty miles away, and have a go at the bank there. And so the men readjusted their plans and went to Northfield to get the lay of the land.

There was only one bank—the First National—overflowing, said Chadwell, with milk and honey. And so the men reconnoitered this new section, as before paying special attention to roads, rivers, and bridges. They decided they would wreck the telegraph office, then gallop off with a bulging bag. It was a splendid idea; the discouragement they had felt after Mankato evaporated and was no more. The lovely, heartwarming sun was out. They would have a successful visit, then head back to wonderful Missouri. Then Cole, with everything taken care of, would head for Texas.

To make doubly sure that everything would be all right, they road into town September 7, 1876, again by twos and threes, and had lunch, also by twos and threes, at different restaurants. Then they rode outside of town and gathered at a spot in the timber three miles from town, and here put the final touches to their plans.

Action. They rode into town in the familiar twos and threes. Through the middle of the town ran the Cannon River, cutting the town in half as neatly as a string through an apple. Cole was to pair with Clell Miller. Frank, Bob Younger, and Charlie Pitts were to be "inside" men. They went ahead, and when Cole and Clell rode across the bridge, the three were sitting on drygoods boxes on the street, gazing at nothing, after the fashion of confirmed loafers. Ambition, however, stirred in them when they saw Cole and Clell, and they got up, and sauntered into the bank. Cole took his position in the middle of the street, dismounted, and pretended to adjust the girth of his saddle, meanwhile looking four directions at once.

Things did not go as they should; in fact, they went very badly, both inside and outside the bank. In no time at all Joseph Lee Heywood, the cashier, was dead and an innocent bystander, as so often happens, also was dead. He was

Nicholas Gustavson, newly arrived from Sweden. Cole called to him, "Get in. Get in," but the young man continued to walk along the street, not understanding what had been said. Cole shot him dead. The other members of the band were shooting right and left to keep the people off the street. But it didn't keep them off. The town sprang to arms; rifles peeped out of windows like guns from a fort. Never, it would seem, had a small town had such a complete arsenal, or, for that matter, such good shots. But, on the other hand, they were using rifles and shotguns, and the men on the street were banging away with pistols, a vast difference. Cole got as close to the door of the bank as he could and shouted, "Come out, boys. They're killing our men," and he was exactly right: Clell Miller lay in the middle of the street, dead as a doornail. And so was Bill Chadwell. Grievously wounded was Jim Younger, shot in the jaw. Frank James came out of the bank; he had killed Cashier Heywood. But when he got outside he had a little trouble himself; he was wounded in the right thigh but was able to get onto the dun horse.

Sprawled on the floor of the bank was the empty grain sack.

In the window fusillade Bob Younger was shot in the elbow. Transferring his pistol to his left hand, he continued to fire. With his arm dangling, he started for his horse; suddenly the horse flinched and fell—dead.

"Get on behind me," Cole called, and this Bob managed to do, the citizens, meanwhile, banging away. No time now to wreck the telegraph office.

"Ride!" shouted Cole, and this the men started to do. Cole's horse with its double burden fell behind. And now the citizens began popping away in earnest. In a marvelous bit of luck Cole and Bob were not hit.

The men had been in town seven minutes. Not a penny had gone into the grain sack.

Four men were dead: the cashier, the boy who could not understand English, Bill Chadwell, and Clell Miller, the boy who admired Jesse and Frank so greatly.

In a few minutes the church bells began to ring and the whistles began to blow. The town was aroused. The six men on the five horses must be taken.

A. E. Bunker, teller at the bank, wrote for publication, August 24, 1894, this incident which would seem to show that not all the citizens of Northfield were heroes:

There was a Norwegian tailor in Northfield named Hamre who had a shop in a basement on the next street south of the bank. He was, this day, walking along Division Street when he saw horsemen and heard shooting and yelling. The tailor waved defiantly at one of the robbers and called, "Come on. Come on." The robber accepted the invitation and rode toward the tailor who ran like mad to his cellar shop and leaped into it. Afterward he said, "I vas not scart. I thought my wife might be narvous and I runned to the shop to tell her effrything vas all right."

CHAPTER XI

What Happened to the Three Who Fell

A<small>ND</small> <small>NOW</small> <small>A</small> few words about what happened to Charlie Pitts. It will be remembered he was the dark-complexioned one who had a mass of black hair, a heavy mustache, and a goatee; he was a bandit and looked the part. Well, I have seen his ear! It reposes in a museum in Northfield, in a glass cage, and can be seen by anyone who yearns to see what a bandit's ear looks like.

Here's the ear story:

It was the law in Minnesota, at this time, that unclaimed bodies would go to the surgeon general of the state. And so the order came through to ship Charlie Pitts to St. Paul. But before he went somebody whacked off an ear as a souvenir.

It happened that a young student from Rush Medical College in Chicago was in St. Paul. He heard that the body was there and asked Dr. Frank W. Murphy, the surgeon general, if he could have Charlie. Dr. Murphy said he could have what was left of Charlie, as the medical students had been whacking away at him.

It also chanced that there was a young practicing doctor in St. Paul named Henry F. Hoyt, who said that he wanted Charlie Pitts's skeleton to hang up in his office to scare the living daylights out of children. At this time nearly every doctor had a skeleton in his closet. But, first, Dr. Hoyt wanted to whiten the bones; the way to do this was to put them in water. An offer of a job in Las Vegas, New Mexico came along, so Dr. Hoyt took all that was left of Charlie Pitts, put him in a box, put the box into a boat, and rowed out on the south branch of Lake Como, just inside the city limits of St. Paul. There he weighted the box with stones, dropped it overboard, and silently rowed away. Then he left for Las Vegas, to be gone a year, Charlie, meanwhile, dutifully whitening. This was in March 1877.

Something new enters. There was a young fellow in St. Paul named August Robertson who liked to hunt muskrats in winter. On this particular day he took with him a hatchet to chop open the ice; through the hole he could spear any luckless muskrat that was passing. As he was walking over the ice, peering through it, he saw something that certainly wasn't a muskrat. It was a box! The stones had slid to one end; the other was tilted up so that it was near the ice.

The boy gave a gasp. Buried treasure!

He got down on his knees, and began to chop with a hearty good will. Finally he was able to reach into the cool depths of the water and edge the box out on the ice. Then he pried off the top of the box and there, before his astonished eyes, was a skeleton!

Leaving the box on the ice, he hurried as fast as he could to the sheriff and told him the shocking story. The sheriff called the coroner and the three hastened to the lake. There was the box and there was the skeleton, exactly as the young muskrat hunter had asserted.

The newspapers seized upon the story of foul murder. People were shocked that such a dreadful thing could happen in their model city. The police said, "We'll soon have the guilty man."

Day after day passed. Nothing happened.

The newspapers began to pummel the police, demanding,

in the name of all law-abiding citizens, action. The police said, "We are making progress and expect soon to make an important announcement."

Time passed.

The papers demanded afresh that something be done. The police said, "We have new important clues."

No arrests. The people became more and more indignant, demanding a "clean up" of the police department. The police said, "The public can expect an arrest in a few days."

A friend in St. Paul sent a clipping about the gruesome murder to young Dr. Hoyt in Las Vegas. Dr. Hoyt knew they were his bones. He would have to get out of the scandal he had stirred up as best he could, and so home he went. He went to the chief of police, and told what had happened. The police verified the story and announced that it had solved the mystery, just as it had promised it would in the beginning, and that once more the people of St. Paul could feel safe in their homes.

Young Dr. Hoyt took the bones to Chicago, where they disappeared, and no one today knows what happened to them. And so ends the career of Charlie Pitts, the toughest of the tough.

And now a few words about Clell Miller, who was the clown, the hearty laugher, the most popular person in the group. His father arrived in Northfield, claimed the body, and took it back home where it was buried beside his blacksmith grandfather Moses Miller. And that was the end of boyish, good-natured Clell Miller who came along to "see the fun."

Bill Chadwell. He was the one who led them into Minnesota with his honey promises. He will be remembered as the little fellow who was the "talker" of the group, the man who never seemed to run down—a sharp contrast, as has been pointed out, to silent Charlie Pitts who talked only when he had something to say. Bill Chadwell didn't have much to say, but that didn't keep him from saying it at length.

Chadwell was shot by a young medical student named Henry W. Wheeler, home on a vacation from Ann Arbor, Michigan. When Chadwell's body was picked up off the street, Wheeler asked if it could be turned over to him; this was granted, and off went the body to the University of Michigan where the boy was a senior.

The body, when it arrived, was delivered by an express wagon after class hours. Wheeler was struggling to get the box into the dissecting room when a freshman—green to the campus—happened along. "Please help me with this," said Wheeler.

The freshman laid hold and the box was finally got into the dissecting room. The freshman looked at the strange sights and sniffed the strange smells. Then he looked more carefully at the box which was beginning to send up an odor. "What is this?" he asked suspiciously.

"It's a man," whispered Wheeler.

The student was shocked. "H—how d-did you get him?"

"I shot him," said Wheeler.

The freshman's eyes rolled and he backed out of the dissecting room and was out of sight in no time.

Chadwell was used for dissecting purposes, and when the senior finished he went to Grand Forks, North Dakota, and there set up an office. And there went the late Bill Chadwell, now an articulated skeleton hanging ingloriously on a hook. There was a piece in the newspapers to the effect that Dr. Wheeler had in his office the skeleton of one of the Northfield outlaws. A short time after this an elderly man appeared at Dr. Wheeler's office. When Dr. Wheeler asked the man into the inside office, the man was ill at ease and said, "I didn't come for medicine. I read you had the remains of a man found on the street in Northfield. Is that true?"

"Yes."

"Could I see it?"

Dr. Wheeler showed him the skeleton. The man was visibly affected and asked some questions. "That's my boy. When we read in the papers what had happened, Ma—that's the boy's mother—said, 'I believe that's our boy. Now you go an' make sure.' I'm convinced it is. Now I'll have to go back and tell her it is our boy hangin' here in your office."

The man did not ask to recover the skeleton and there it remained many years.

CHAPTER XII

The Great Man Hunt. Jesse James Threatens to Kill Cole's Brother. Hanska Slough Yields Them Up

THE MISSOURI men set out on the kind of ride they knew so well. Never in all their years had they been overtaken by a posse. So things would go all right this time. But never before had they left two of their men on the ground.

The Northfield men caught the two horses left by the bandits. There was a great dashing to and fro; soon four men came clattering up on horses, armed with fowling pieces. And now the six started after the Missouri men, determined to shoot them down and get the matter over with. They had outshot them in Northfield, but the Northfield men had rifles and shotguns and were in buildings. Now it would be a bit different. The six, riding like the wind, caught up with the Missouri men who promptly began to fire. In no time all the Northfield boys decided to go back and get other men and let them share the honors with them. And back they went, almost as fast as they had come. Meanwhile, the telegraph key in Northfield was chattering away.

Bob Younger was holding on to Cole as best he could, and then came a bit of luck. The two met a farmer jogging along to town in a spring wagon with a team of horses. Before he knew what was happening, the farmer had only one horse.

But even alone on a horse it was rough riding for Bob without a saddle.

They came to a farm where a farmer was standing near the barn. Cole rode up to him.

"Hello there. We're officers of the law and we're chasin' horse thieves. Our man here left so hastily that he did not have time to get a saddle. Can you loan him one? We'll come back this way and return it."

"I'd be pleased to," said the farmer, delighted to be of service to his community.

The saddle was clapped on.

Away Cole and the others clattered, hard upon the trail of the low-down horse thieves.

But all was not well. Bob had ridden only three or four miles when the saddle girth broke and pitched him off. Bob got up, his arm dangling helplessly and tried to catch the animal. He did not succeed, and so once more he got up behind Cole.

They came to another farmhouse and told their story. The farmer said yes, by all means take his horse and saddle. Bob mounted thankfully, but the horse balked and no amount of persuasion could make him stir. So down came poor Bob and up again behind Cole. They soon saw a farmer and another barn. Now grown desperate, the two went to the farmer and, without any noble talk, grabbed a horse and a saddle and down the road the two went, hurrying like mad to catch up with the others.

Finally the men came to a small family hotel in Shieldsville where they stopped to get something to eat. They tied their horses and started in, when they saw something that made their eyes pop. Leaning against the porch railing was a whole line of rifles and muskets, and, inside, eating, was a posse. Cole and his men tiptoed silently away, mounted their horses, and started wearily on again.

What they were beginning to be aware of was that the whole state had been alerted, thanks to the little key, and that a dozen posses were looking for them, with instructions to shoot first, then ask. The police chiefs of St. Paul and Minneapolis had sent men; every sheriff and deputy in the state knew by now it was the James-Younger gang and that a reward was on every man taken, dead or alive. Trains were filled with man hunters and still more were coming; there were 900 after the six. The only clue the hunters had was that the outlaws were working west and south toward Missouri; and so men were rushed to get ahead of the outlaws and throw out a net. The outlaws slipped through, like minnows through a whale net. The Pinkertons came and joined in, accomplishing nothing. In all their years of trailing Jesse and Frank they hadn't even seen them.

It was the biggest man hunt the press had ever had a whack at. The *St. Paul Pioneer Press* sent a reporter on an early morning train, September 8, and at nine o'clock on that date he was attached to what was called a "pursuit party" commanded by Colonel Wheeler. The reporter wrote his first dispatch bravely. "Headquarters: in the saddle," it said. He saw nothing. Finally, on the third day, he went back to Mankato and sat on the porch waiting for something to happen.

The Missourians were outdistancing the hunters and were on the homeward trail when an unexpected thing happened: rain. At first this wasn't too depressing, but instead of letting up, the rain kept coming down. This part of Minnesota was close to the swamps and now the horses began to mire down in the terrible morass. They must have fresh horses. They found a farmer and asked him if he wanted to trade. He said he didn't. But he traded anyway, and was glad to do so.

On top of it all, Bob's arm was paining him more and more. And it was seen that Jim Younger had been wounded worse than it was at first realized. The bullet had swept away part of his jawbone and he was losing blood.

That night the little group found a dry spot on a kind of spongy mound in the swamp, spread their horse blankets over some bushes, and crawled in to rest and sleep. The next morning they decided they would abandon the horses and set out on foot through the maddening, cruel, endless swamp. Leaving their horses tied where they would probably be rescued, the six men wearily set out. Not a shot had been fired at them since they had left Northfield.

Five days passed.

Then they heard the pursuers.

The courage of the outlaws was almost unbelievable. Nothing was too overwhelming to keep them from trying.

Their humanity toward the horses cost them dearly. The posse found the horses. This changed everything. Instead of looking for men on horseback, they sent out word to search for men on foot. A new shipment of hunters was rushed in, as the first ones had become tired and weary.

A man who had been a general in the Civil War, E. M. Pope, was sent for. He would know how to take the six. "We'll soon get them," he said when he took command. He spoke a trifle too confidently, for during all the time he was in command he never even saw them.

Now and then the outlaws saw the hunters, who were coming closer and closer. Jim Younger was stumbling along, growing weaker.

At last they felt they had outdistanced their pursuers and they experienced a great wave of thankfulness. They came to Mankato—the very place where they had started—and began to creep through town like shadows. They passed Bierbauer's Brewery and came to Boegan's Lumber Mill and were moving silently past it when suddenly there was a terrific blast of a whistle. The flabbergasted men began to run, for they thought they had been discovered and that the whistle was a signal to arouse the town. As a matter of fact it was the twelve-o'clock midnight whistle, which was sounded for the night shift. But the men didn't know it and ran stumbling on. Finally they came to the railroad bridge over Le Sueur River and thankfully got across. Now they would be safe.

But soon they heard the hunters. The men continued to stumble along as best they could, overcoming almost impossible obstacles. Jim Younger was growing weaker. Jesse studied him, then made a sign for Cole to follow. Cole did. When they were out of Jim's hearing, Jesse said in a low voice, "We'll have to do something about Jim."

"What do you mean?" asked Cole.

"You know what I mean. He's holding us up and we may all be captured."

"He's doing the best he can," protested Cole.

"It's either him or us. I'm going to shoot him."

"If you shoot him, I'll kill you," said Cole, drawing his pistol. The two men faced each other silently. "I'll call Frank," Cole said.

Cole called Frank James and told him what Jesse had said. "We're not going to kill Jim, nor anyone else," Frank said to Jesse.

Jesse went off by himself, surly and resentful. And now Cole had to watch Jesse every moment, for Jesse was not a man to be put aside.

It was a game that Cole had played many times during guerrilla days—hunter and hunted—but never had he played it so long or with so many men against him. And on top of it all with Jesse, who seemed to be watching his chance.

Finally Jesse went up to Cole and said, "You see how things are going. We've got to split."

The six men discussed it for some time, and then came the division—the James brothers would stay together and take their chances, and the Younger brothers would stick together. Rough, tough Charlie Pitts would stay with Cole. "Good luck," said Jesse, and then he and Frank slopped off through the swamp.

After a short rest the four got up and plodded off together. They found some ears of field corn, some turnips, potatoes, and some stalks of sorghum which they chewed. They saw a chicken but did not dare to shoot it. They continued to press along in their wet clothes and in their wet boots, for they had all worn boots, after the style of land and cattle buyers of the day.

As they struggled along, they saw a farmer driving a team hitched to a light wagon. Horses! The four men, delighted by this unexpected luck, ran stumbling toward the farmer.

"Wait a minute," shouted Charlie Pitts. "We want to borrow your horses. We're officers looking for the Northfield bank robbers."

The farmer gazed over his shoulder at the sorry-looking men, seized his whip, lashed the horses into a run, and was soon gone.

One would think, under the stress of day-and-night pursuit, that the men would begin to quarrel among themselves and to blame each other for things that went wrong, but instead they were kind and considerate of each other. Of course two of the men were Cole's brothers, but even with a third man among them, all four worked in utmost harmony, with no quarrels and no bickering. If they had to die, they would die together, each man doing his part.

The pursuers seemed to be drawing closer; Cole listened for dogs, but did not hear them. Their hopes began to revive. They would make it. They would get away. Suddenly a volley was discharged at them by men they hadn't even seen. Cole and the three ran for a stretch of timber and hid themselves, waiting.

The pursuers would advance a little, then wait, maddeningly out of sight. Then, suddenly, another volley would ring out. Cole was wounded again, but he kept going, and so did the others. Nothing should stop them. If they got out of Hanska Slough they would be safe, they thought. Day after day they kept working southwestward, with the pursuers relentlessly after them. When one posse tired out, another took its place. There was no stopping day or night. Meantime, it was raining day after day. Their clothes were never dry.

Cole became so weak that he cut himself a staff and leaned on it to help him through the swamp. The pursuers knew short cuts where there were dry paths.

Then came the most dreadful, the most heartbreaking moment of all. The four weary men saw a fresh group of seven getting ready to charge. The possemen fired a round. A bullet cut the staff Cole had been leaning on, and he staggered and fell. But in a moment he was able to get to his feet.

"Surrender, or we will kill you," shouted the leader of the posse.

The four fired at the posse.

The leader of the posse formed his seven in a line, eight feet apart, and shouted, "Forward! Fire along the whole line." The four men hiding in the mire saw them coming and managed to fire. Almost instantly the seven fired. Charlie Pitts groaned. In a moment he was dead.

And now the three brothers were alone, all wounded, all weak, all courageous.

"Surrender, or you die!" shouted the captain.

The brothers whispered together, then Bob Younger got unsteadily to his feet, his wounded arm in a muddy sling. "Don't fire. All of our men are down except me."

With drawn rifles the posse approached. In a moment the three were prisoners.

The possemen were astonished to see in what a pitiful condition the outlaws were, and how they had stood up under fire. Cole had been wounded eleven times. Jim Younger had been wounded five times. Bob Younger had been wounded four times.

One of the men in the posse was Thomas L. Vought and now, as he came closer to the prisoners, he stared at Cole very hard. "Aren't you the man who stopped at my hotel?"

"I had the honor," said Cole who, even in this black moment, had a sense of humor.

"Where's your partner?"

"We left him in Northfield."

A runner left for Madelia, six miles away, with the exciting news: the brave posse had captured the bandits. And soon the news was all over Minnesota, and, for that matter, all over the United States.

One of the posse got a light spring wagon from a farmer, Charlie Pitts was tossed in, and the three brothers were helped into the wagon where they sat on the floor beside the body of Charlie Pitts. The wagon and the posse started to Madelia. "Did Frank and Jesse get away?" Cole asked.

"Yes," one of the men said.

A look of relief came over Cole's face, for his loyalty to Frank was touching.

The word had spread. When the wagon got to Madelia, the streets were filled with people who wanted to see the dangerous men. The sheriff allowed the captured men to stay in the town only a brief time, then put them on a train for Faribault, which had an escape-proof jail.

There were five guards over the three brothers. So dangerous did the guards believe the brothers to be, the brothers were placed in different seats with a guard beside each wounded man. One of the guards was Theodore Edgar Potter, who lived one mile from Garden City on the Wattonwan River, Minnesota. Later he wrote his autobiography for his children. It was published in 1913 by the Rumford Press, Concord, New Hampshire. He had no reason to tell anything except the truth. In the book he relates this incident:

J. J. Shaubut, who was vice-president of the bank in Mankato that the men had started to rob, came up and sat down near Cole. On being told who the banker was, Cole said, "I hear the two James brothers have been killed and that we are all that is left of the eight who visited your city fifteen days ago."

The banker began to lecture Cole, saying, "You and all the others are a despicable gang and a disgrace to our country."

Cole, although worn and weary, roused himself. "Wait a minute! This is a question I have given considerable thought to and I would like to ask you—would you like to know the difference between what you do and what I do?"

"Yes."

"It's very simple. You rob the poor and I rob the rich."

The banker got up and left, indignantly sputtering.

A great crowd met the train in Faribault, and as the

prisoners were helped off, the people stared hard at the dangerous men. The prisoners were taken to the Flanders House, Cole, this time, nonpaying. A doctor was called and he put Cole and Bob into the same bed.

Cole began to complain of his feet. "I want to take off my boots," he said.

When the boots were removed, the nails on both his big toes came off.

The doctor turned his attention to Jim Younger, whose jaw had been shot away. The doctor probed for some moments, then pulled out a segment of the jawbone; on it were two teeth.

After this medical attention the doctor allowed the curiosity seekers waiting downstairs to file through the room and look at the two dangerous men and then file out, a strange proceeding, indeed.

A Pinkerton detective from St. Paul arrived and looked with interest at the men.

General Pope, who had said, "We'll soon get them," came to the hotel and studied them.

The officers shot questions at the two supine men.

"Why did you select the bank in Mankato as the one to rob?"

"Because," said Cole, "we had lost our money in St. Paul to men we found out were crooked professional gamblers, and we wanted to get even with the state."

Cole saw that this question would be asked again, and he thought up a very good answer, indeed; in a way it was a small inspiration. This time he said that a Northern man, General Benjamin F. Butler, had mistreated Southerners in Louisiana during the Civil War and that he, Cole, had heard that General Butler had $75,000 invested in the bank and that they had robbed the bank as an act of revenge.

The Civil War had been over eleven years, but Cole made the revenge motive seem believable. He knew there would be a trial and he meant to use every possible device for him and his brothers to escape the death penalty. He was going to defend himself with all the cunning and cleverness he had used in raiding and robbing.

"Who were the two who got away?" he was asked.

"One was named Howard, the other was named Woods. They joined late and I don't know much about them."

"Why don't you?" one of the officers asked.

"Men who ride don't ask questions."

He chose the name Howard for Jesse, because, from time to time, Jesse had used the name himself. He chose the name Woods for Frank because Jesse's middle name was Woodson, and Cole divided it in half, adding an *s*. It was quick thinking. Would these distortions pile up against him? That was the question.

He had changed his story. Would that operate against him?

Cole had expected the citizens to be enraged against him and his brothers and he thought they might even rush the jail, but instead of this the people were only curious. Some sympathy even went to them; after all, they were only six and then four and there had, at the top, been 900 pursuers. And some of the pursuers had not been too eager to close with the bandits, human nature being what it is. Of course two of the citizens of Northfield had given up their lives; that was shocking. But the bandits also had lost two. And now when the people saw the Youngers face to face, the Youngers were not fierce at all, but, on the whole, rather likable. Cole was the spokesman; he talked well and he made a favorable impression. But he would not talk about the two men who had escaped.

Cole presented a side that was completely new to his captors. He said if it had not been for the Civil War that he and his brothers would not have taken up arms against the law. He spoke of the high position his family had held in Missouri and of the importance of his father, and he told how his mother had been burned out in the winter. In addition he was contrite and asked the people to pray for him— a little of an actor there. But whatever it took to escape hanging, he meant to use.

The three gained rapidly. Cole was walking without a limp. Jim could talk more plainly, but could not chew solid food. Bob was not suffering so much. The day of the hearing came. The three were shackled together—Cole in the middle —and led from the jail in Faribault to the courthouse.

Their sister, Miss Retta Younger, who was a good-looking girl of seventeen, came into the courtroom and saw her three brothers. She began to weep, and so did the brothers.

The three Youngers faced the grand jury at Faribault on four charges:

1. The murder of Heywood.
2. The murder of the Swede.
3. Robbery of the bank.
4. Assault on A. E. Bunker, teller.

The brothers realized there was every chance they would be sentenced to hang, but they also knew there was a law in Minnesota that a person who pleads guilty cannot be put to death. Such a person could get a life sentence, but that was all. Cole and his brothers made up their minds to plead guilty.

When the moment came for the jury to render its verdict, the brothers were brought in, shackled together. "We find the defendants guilty," said the foreman.

The judge was so affected that for a moment he could not

speak. Women sobbed; one woman got into the aisle and began pushing toward the prisoners, saying she wanted to kiss them.

Cole determined that somehow he and his brothers would get out of prison and once more be free men. Just how he would manage this he didn't know, but some way or other he would bring it about.

Meantime, Jesse and Frank had escaped. They had got to Nebraska and by train had gone to Missouri where they had tucked themselves away so many times. But the country had been so aroused against them that they did not feel safe in Missouri and so, under other names and disguises, they went to Tennessee. The Pinkertons continued to look for them, but found them not.

CHAPTER XIII

Belle Starr Becomes Ruler of Younger's Bend. Belle Mourns Cole in Her Own Way. Her Strange Death

BELLE STARR was shocked when she heard that Cole had been taken, and soon she learned that he had been sentenced to life imprisonment. Pearl's father!

Belle's life had been a full one. She was twenty-eight. She had been a spy for the Confederacy, and she had had one great romance, and from this a child. She had been legitimately married and from this marriage a son—"Eddie" Reed. Once she wrote in a letter: "I don't think there is a more intelligent boy living." But the boy's father was now in a pauper's graveyard. And Pearl's father in prison. On top of all this, Belle's parents were constantly critical of Pearl's nameless position; the family held back no words in speaking of Pearl's parentage and now, with Cole in prison, matters grew worse than ever. Pearl would never see her father again, they said, and began to call the child "Rosie" Reed. But Belle would have none of this; the child was Pearl Younger and Pearl Younger she would remain.

A piece of good luck happened; at least it seemed to be good luck. Belle's father and mother moved to Dallas. Belle's escape from her troubles was to become a faro dealer in a gambling house. Dallas at this time was a wide-open, high-kicking town. Dealing faro was not a perfect job, but at least it got her away from her critical family with their slurs on Pearl. Belle was not too good-looking, but she had nice eyes and nice hair. In fact, any woman in a gambling room was, to the hungry-eyed men, an enchanting creature. She had a personality and was quick in the rough repartee of the period and was considered jolly. In addition, she could play the piano, something that few other women decorating the frontier saloons could do.

Soon she had a horse of her own, and this she liked to ride up and down the streets of Dallas, dressed in the extreme style of the period. And as she rode in her sidesaddle she had two pistols buckled around her waist. Part of this display was showmanship, for there was no instance during this period that she used them. In a way, she was an actress. She liked to attract attention and to "put on a show." When she got home, matters were not quite so glamorous, for there was her critical, complaining father. She was disgracing him and was "running" with people who were sure to get her into trouble, he said. But in her recklessness Belle went her way. She could manage her own life.

One day as Belle was dealing faro she was startled to see Jesse James in the crowd watching the game. He had evidently been waiting for her to catch his eye, for he gave her a look that meant for her to show no sign of recognition, and to come to him as soon as she could. He moved away, and soon she followed. How much had happened since a day years ago when he had ridden up with Frank James and Cole. He was well known then; now he was famous from one end of America to the other.

He seated himself, his back to the wall, on one of the benches that ran along the side of the room. The slap of the cards on the table and the click of the dice filled the room, the sound rising and falling. Now and then there was a curse; sometimes there was a sharp, triumphant laugh.

When Belle got to study him carefully he seemed more nervous than ever; he had always been nervous, but now his nervousness was more pronounced; he moved his eyes constantly, looking first here and then there. But he still had the same clear, flashing blue eyes—eyes that could grow so cold and cruel and deadly.

"I wanted to see you," he said. "I thought maybe you'd like to know what happened."

"I do," she said eagerly.

"It was bad." As Jesse spoke, a man passed; Jesse watched him silently and did not speak until the man was out of hearing. "Frank and I managed to escape, as you know. Three of our men are dead. I never did want to go to Minnesota," he added bitterly. "Cole didn't either, for that matter. He's in for life. I guess you know that, too. But he may get out. I hope so."

"I hope so, too," Belle said fervently.

Another man walked by. Jesse waited until the man had gone. "You never know," he said. "I have to keep moving all the time. It's not like the old days, where I could pull in with my friends in Missouri and Kentucky. People don't want to take me in any more. The papers tell where I've robbed a bank or a train—and I haven't been there at all. That helps throw them off!" He laughed mockingly. "I'll never be taken alive. I've made up my mind to that." His voice was full of feeling, for he was speaking of something deep within him. "Never."

They continued to talk. Finally Jesse stood up. "I'll have to go," he said, and left without telling her where he was going.

Belle went back to the table, and again started to deal, but her mind was on what Jesse had told her. There must, she thought, be a way to get Cole out.

About this time she fell in with Blue Duck, whose name was not unusual in the Indian Territory where there were Black Hawks and Grey Eagles. He was born in the Cherokee Nation in 1862, and was three quarters Cherokee and fourteen years younger than Belle. He was hardly able to read or write, but was considered handsome, even a bit dashing. Belle, who had once associated with the best people in Jasper County, Missouri, began to associate with Blue Duck. She had sunk so low that the two of them began to steal cattle—something that Belle would never have dreamed of doing back in Missouri.

And now happened an incident that is always told about Belle—a peculiar and spectacular one. The story, in its details, was passed on to me by Mrs. Zoe A. Tilghman, widow of Bill Tilghman, the famous United States deputy marshal. Bill Tilghman never knew Belle, but he knew so many men who did know her that he himself accepted the tale:

Belle and Blue Duck brought some stolen cattle to Dodge City where they disposed of them. Blue Duck was electrified by the sight of so much money—$1,800—and was filled with the desire to add to it. He went to a gambling room which was up a flight of steps, located on the second floor, over the main establishment. Well, he didn't add to it. In fact, in no time he was plucked as clean as a Christmas goose.

Shamefaced, he went back to Belle and confessed that he had lost their money. She was indignant—strangely enough not at him but at the crooked faro dealers.

"I'm going there and see about it," she said.

The two brought their horses as close as they could to the gambling hall. "Hold them till I get back," she said, "then be prepared to move fast."

Going up the stairs in her rugged cowboy outfit, she peeped through the door, studied the layout, then walked boldly in, pointed her six-shooter at the faro dealer, and said, "I'll take the money on the board."

The players, some heavy with liquor, looked at her in startled surprise, not knowing whether it was a crude joke or if she meant it. They soon found out that she meant it, for she brought out a grain sack, after the immemorial way of the West, and began dumping the money into it. Then she backed out, gun in one hand, grain sack in the other, and was out the door before the men had had time to gain their wits. Even if they had gained them, they probably would not have attempted to shoot her, so important, so sought after were women in the wild West. Anyway, in no time at all Belle was down the stairs, with about $3,000 in her grain sack, and in a moment more she and Blue Duck were riding like the wind.

I am inclined to believe the story.

Blue Duck later got himself into a bit of trouble: he killed a man, a matter not looked on with approval even in turbulent Indian Territory. In a short time he was up before Isaac C. Parker, the Hanging Judge of Arkansas. Judge Parker heard the case and said that Blue Duck would have to hang just like anyone else and sentenced him, April 30, 1886. Belle raised money, got Lawyer J. Warren Reed, threw dust in all directions, and finally got the president of the United States to commute Blue Duck's sentence to life imprisonment. No penitentiary in Arkansas was considered suitable for taking care of him, so Blue Duck was bundled up and sent to the Southern Illinois Penitentiary at Menard, Illinois. When asked by the records officer if he was married he said no. The answer was correct, but it didn't fully cover the situation. And there he remained until March 20, 1895, when he was pardoned and walked out a free man. But Belle was not there to meet him. And thus ended the romance between Belle and Blue Duck. It would seem that Belle took up with her murderous admirer when she was low in her mind about Cole. Anyway, it was one of the strange episodes in her strange life.

Through Blue Duck she had become acquainted with a wild, desolate, forbidding section on the South Canadian River in the Indian Territory which was the habitat of cattle thieves, horse thieves, whisky peddlers, train robbers, and other wanted men. Travelers who started through it never got across. She met the man who ruled this section— Tom Starr, the most dangerous, the cruelest Indian in the Territory. He was head of the biggest Indian family in the Cherokee Nation; even today they are a numerous family.

In fact, the year I was working on this book the Starrs gathered at Porum for the first family reunion. Under the direction of Tom Starr's great-great-granddaughters—Ruth, Elmire, and Rose Starr—the family cleared off the ancient graves of the Starrs, which had become covered by a heavy undergrowth of wild vines. But they did not go to Belle Starr's grave, which was only a short distance away, for they did not want to bring attention to her. On Sunday 120 descendants of Tom Starr walked among the graves, and then went to the church where the minister preached in Cherokee. The younger members of the clan did not understand their tribal language and so an interpreter stood beside the preacher and translated into English. When services were over, the descendants came out and stood in the little country churchyard talking, some in English, some in Cherokee. It was a touching meeting, this reunion of one of the great Indian families.

Tom Starr was six feet, five inches tall, thick-shouldered,

with coarse black hair and unusually large feet. When he talked, it was with a sort of snarl. Everyone was afraid of him, and well they might be. Once, when he was carrying on a feud with a family, he set fire to the neighbor's house. A little boy, aged about six, came running out and begged Tom Starr not to burn down the house. "Come here, little boy," said Tom Starr in a kindly voice. He picked up the child and tossed him into the flames.

If Belle knew this, it did not deter her. She went to Tom Starr's cabin six miles south of Briartown, and there met Tom's son Sam Starr, who was six feet tall but, in contrast to his father, light-complexioned, handsome, and soft-voiced.

Belle had two children to think of. She made herself agreeable to the handsome Indian. The result was inevitable. Finally Belle asked for marriage, not only for social approval but because Sam, by tribal allotment, had sixty acres of land.

Research turns up the following from the Canadian County, Cherokee Nation, records, Vol. 1 B, page 297:

"*Marriage Report*. On the 5th day of June, 1880, by Abe Woodall, District Judge for Canadian District, Cherokee Nation. Samuel Starr, a citizen of the Cherokee Nation, age 23 years, and Mrs. Belle Reed, a citizen of the United States, age 27 years.

H. J. Vann, Clerk."

Sam probably gave his correct age, for he had no reason to hide it and was among people who had always known him. Belle, however, exercised a woman's prerogative and came out of the hopper five years younger than she really was. But there she was—married to a full-blooded Cherokee nine years younger than herself. Belle had had three husbands, but this was the first one she had ever got into the written record. Anyway, once again Pearl Younger and Eddie Reed had a daddy, unusual a parent as Sam was.

The two then went off on what was no doubt a belated honeymoon.

Pearl, when this happy event took place, was eleven, Eddie, nine.

For the looks of things, Belle began to call her daughter Pearl Starr. Cole had been in prison now for four years. Belle was sending money to help get him out.

Belle and Sam immediately set up in business—a very profitable one in that section: horse stealing. A horse was still a man's most valuable personal property, something akin, later, to a car. The two sold their horses to middlemen; some of the horses went to Texas, some to Kansas, some to Missouri. The two also stole cattle—also a nice-paying business.

They soon became the most prosperous couple in the section. Belle took a fancy to the part that was wildest and most inaccessible and was able to buy a stretch of land in a loop of the South Canadian River, and gave it, in honor of Cole, the name Younger's Bend. And in it today is a white wooden country schoolhouse usually called the Cole Younger School, but officially Younger's Bend School. And Younger's Bend this section still is, still inaccessible, still wild and sinister.

The cabin had been occupied by Big Head, a Cherokee. When Belle took possession she immediately began to enlarge the cabin; at first it had only one room; soon it had three.

The place was admirably fitted for horse work. No officer of the law could get within miles of the place without the word reaching Belle; so much for her newly acquired family who didn't like strangers no how. In addition there was a cave where Belle and her friends could hide their horses, and a spring where they could water them. Before one could arrive at Belle's honeymoon cottage there was a steep, sharp-walled canyon where an unpiloted person could break his neck.

At first she began to shelter a few friends—men on whom the law had fixed its eye. Then she began to take in more until in no time Younger's Bend had more outlaws in hiding than had any other place in the United States. In fact, it still holds the record. The place was called "Robbers' Roost"; the name fitted it as a cartridge does its barrel. Belle became their guiding spirit—their "brains," as it was put. And she rode with them, helping rob and plunder, this once refined girl. Since she had parted from Cole her moral fiber had weakened and she was doing things now that once she would have been ashamed to do. But, on the other hand, she did not want Pearl to lead the kind of life that she herself was following. She wanted, as she herself put it, for Pearl to be a "lady." She called her "the Canadian Lily."

Belle was mistress in her home but ruled it in a kindly fashion. One Saturday night Sam and three of his cronies were having a poker game when they got into an argument that became so heated that one of the men threatened to shoot one of the others. Belle listened for some minutes, then said, "I'm tired of all this squabbling. Real men don't threaten to kill each other over a poker game. Sam, give me your gun."

Sam fished it out.

Belle took it, locked it up in a strongbox where she kept her valuables, and said, "It's going to stay there until you go to church, and to prove you've been there you've got to bring back a hymnbook."

The men stopped their quarreling and the game continued pleasantly.

The next day the church in Porum had a worshiper whom many said they had never seen there before.

However, Belle still had great affection for Cole. This might have been a recollection of their romantic days together, but whatever it was, she was still in love with him. The other men who had come and gone in her life had made little impression. Cole remained. But after Cole's imprisonment, she kept her thoughts to herself. Though she now called her daughter Pearl Starr, in legal matters she was "Pearl Younger." In 1886 Belle was brought before Judge Parker's court, in Fort Smith, Arkansas, on a charge of horse stealing. The man who made the complaint was Albert McCarty. Belle went to the court and filed a petition asking that the government subpoena her witnesses as she was not able to do so herself. The petition was approved by Isaac C. Parker, February 8, 1886. His signature can be seen today on the document. One of her witnesses was Pearl Younger, who was then seventeen, and there, on the document, her name appears with a statement as to what she can swear to in court. Another witness was Edwin Reed who, the petition says, "lives in Vian district, Cherokee Nation, seventy miles west of Fort Smith by train." It is believed that both Pearl and Edwin Reed testified for their mother; at least Belle proved herself innocent of stealing the horse and all was well. This, so far as I can find, is the only court record attesting that her daughter was Pearl Younger.

Belle's and Sam's business had a rude interruption. Judge Parker wanted to see both of them this time about a matter of horse stealing. The indictment read that she was "the leader of a band of horse thieves."

L. W. Marks, Vinita, Oklahoma, who was a United States deputy marshal working out of Judge Parker's court, told the story of what happened:

He, with another deputy, was sent to arrest Belle and Sam, but so perfect was Belle's organization that the word promptly got to Belle and Sam, and the two dusted out. Marks and his deputy turned up the scent and went to the cabin in the Osage Hills where they believed Belle and Sam were hiding. The cabin was occupied by a Negro family, and Belle and Sam had stayed overnight with them.

The officers concealed themselves till morning. Shortly after dawn Sam and a Negro boy, who seemed to be the only male at home, came out to water and feed the horses. The two officers hid behind a corncrib, then popped out and made Sam and the Negro boy prisoners. Then they ordered the Negro boy to go back to the cabin and tell Belle that Sam had been kicked by a horse, and to come as fast as she could. The men said if the boy didn't do exactly as they ordered, they would arrest him and take him to Fort Smith before Judge Parker.

The boy returned to the house and in no time at all Belle came hurrying out in a kind of nightdress. The officers grabbed Belle, who fought like a tiger. But the men subdued her. Then, to their astonishment, they found that she had a six-shooter in a pocket in her nightdress and two derringers in the bosom of her blouse. "I'll kill you yet!" she shouted.

After breakfast the officers put Belle and Sam into the prison wagon and started to Fort Smith. Along with Belle and Sam were two other prisoners, all riding in the prison wagon, after the way things were managed at this time in the Indian Territory.

Belle was so mad that, as the wagon rolled along, she

began to drop out the knives and forks and tins that the officers used to cook with, also the blankets used for camping. When they drew up that night and started to get supper, the officers were almost as mad as Belle. They got along as best they could, but the next day she began to throw out other things. Finally the officers had to take her to the front end of the wagon and chain her there, out of reach of their camping equipment. That night they chained her to a wagon wheel. A blanket was spread on the ground and thus, one ankle secured to the wheel, Belle slept, still mad.

Finally she arrived at Fort Smith and soon appeared in Judge Parker's famous court. Belle and Sam were sentenced to a year each in prison in Detroit. This was the first time a woman had ever been sent up as a horse thief—let alone as a leader of horse thieves—and the newspapers hopped onto the story with shouts of glee. And so did the *National Police Gazette*. She was now the most noted woman bandit America had ever produced; much of it started that day in the courtroom in Arkansas.

Pearl was now fourteen, a rather pretty girl—the girl that Belle wanted to become a "lady." Before she left for prison, Belle is alleged to have written the following letter, addressed, according to Harman, to Miss Pearl Younger, Oswego, Kansas:

Pandemonium, Feb.—1883

Baby Pearl,

My dear little one. It is useless to attempt to conceal my trouble from you and though you are nothing but a child I have confidence that my darling will bear with fortitude what I now write.

I shall be away from you for a few months, baby, and have only this consolation to offer you, that never again will I be placed in such humiliating circumstances and that in the future your little tender heart shall never more ache, or a blush called to your cheek on your mother's account. Sam and I were tried here, John West the main evidence against us. We were found guilty and sentenced to a year at the House of Correction, Detroit, Michigan, for which place we start in the morning. Now Pearl there is a vast difference in that place and a penitentiary; you must bear that in mind, and not think of mama being shut up in a gloomy prison. It is said to be one of the finest institutions in the United States, surrounded by beautiful grounds, with fountains and everything nice. There I can have my education renewed, and I stand sadly in need of it. Sam will have to attend school and I think it is the best thing that ever happened for him, and now you must not be unhappy and brood over our absence. It wont take the time long to glide by and as we come home we will get you and then we will have such a nice time.

We will get your horse up and I will break him and you can ride John while I am gentling Loco. We will have Eddie with us and will be as gay and happy as the birds we claim at home. Now baby you can either stay with grandma or your Mama Mc, just as you like and do the best you can until I come back, which won't be long. Tell Eddie that he can go down home with us and have a good time hunting and though I wish not to deprive Marion and ma of him for any length of time, yet I must keep him for a while. Love to ma and Marion.

Uncle Tom has stood by me nobly in our trouble, done everything that any one could do. Now baby I will write to you often. You must write to your grandma, but don't tell her of this; and to your Aunt Ellen, Mama Mc, but to no one else. Remember, I don't care who writes to you, you must not answer. I say this because I do not want you to correspond with anyone in the Indian Territory, my baby, my sweet little one, and you must mind me. Except Auntie; if you wish to hear from me, auntie will let you know. If you should write me, ma would find out where I am and, Pearl, you must never let her know. Her head is overburdened with care now and therefore you must keep this carefully guarded from her.

Destroy this letter as soon as read. As I told you before, if you wish to stay a while with your Mama Mc, I am willing. But you must devote your time to your studies. Bye bye, sweet baby mine.

BELLE STARR

The "Sam" mentioned is her husband, Sam Starr. "Uncle Tom" is Tom Starr, Sam's father. "Eddie" is Belle's son Eddie Reed. I cannot identify Aunt Ellen, Marion, or Mama Mc. See my comments in *Sources*, Chapter 11.

The main thing is that Belle and Sam were off to prison. And Cole was in his prison, too.

Prisoners could get out after serving three-fourths of their term if they were model prisoners. And this Belle and Sam made themselves. In nine months the two were out and back at Younger's Bend, and Pearl and Eddie with them.

The Detroit trip did not teach Belle a lesson. Soon she was in business again. She dressed as a man and rode and robbed. More and more her fortress became a robbers' retreat. Belle made one rule for her visitors: no rough talk in front of the Canadian Lily. Eddie, seeing the men who lived without working, looked on them with more and more approval.

Sam was becoming increasingly wild. The United States marshals were after him, and so were the Cherokee Indian police, the Choctaw Indian police, and the Creek Indian police, the latter most determinedly of all, for Sam had robbed the treasury of the Creek Nation. With Belle's help he managed to elude them. But time was ticking.

Living a mile away was Frank West, a member of the Starr clan and a cousin of Sam Starr. But the two didn't get along. One day Sam was riding along on Belle's mare Venus when a shot rang out. The bullet missed Sam but killed the mare. Sam thought the shot had been fired by Frank West, but, as a matter of fact, it had been fired by a member of the Cherokee Indian police who was trying to get the "drop" on Sam, this also being the way things were managed in the Indian Territory.

One night shortly before Christmas 1886, Mrs. Lucy Suratt gave a "stomp" dance. The dance was to take place in the yard, as all stomp dances did. The tang of winter added to the dance, for the dancers really had to stomp to keep warm. But even this was not enough, so a bonfire was started. The dancers were swaying and swinging and setting their feet down with the jerky movements peculiar to Indians, in time to the beating of the Indian drums. Belle and Sam arrived and, chilly from their horseback ride, started across the yard to the bonfire; as they did so they saw the hated Frank West squatting in front of the fire, warming himself. Belle stepped in front of Sam so that Frank West would not see him. Frank saw Belle but in the darkness did not see Sam. Suddenly Belle stepped aside and Sam fired, hitting Frank West in the neck. Frank swayed uncertainly, then sank to the ground, his hand fumbling in his overcoat pocket. He managed to extract a pistol and, propping himself up on his elbow, fired. Sam swayed back and forth, then staggered toward a tree. Throwing his arms around the tree, he tried to hold himself upright. In a moment his grip loosened and he fell to the ground, dead. Events had happened with lightning swiftness.

The people stood around for some moments, talking about what had happened. A wagon was brought, finally, and the two bodies dumped in and taken to the Starr burying ground near Porum.

With the same lightning swiftness Belle had become a widow. She was now thirty-eight. Her life had been a dramatic one. Cole was in prison. Jim Reed was dead. Blue Duck was in prison, and now Sam Starr was dead.

Belle began to worry about Pearl. The outlaws were making advances to Pearl, who was a pleasant-mannered, likable girl, with black hair, black eyes, and a nose that turned up a little at the end. Her mother warned her against the men, for no one knew evil men better than Belle did, but Pearl liked being the center of attention. Belle engaged a country "fiddler" and had a dance in her cabin, and here the bandits kicked up their heels, each eager to swing Pearl. Belle watched all this. . . . Once she'd been the one the men wanted to swing.

Bandits everywhere in "the Nation," as this part of the Indian Territory was called, knew they would be welcome at Younger's Bend and every few days a horseman would ride out of the timber and halloo. Belle would come to the door, rifle in hand, and ask who it was. One of the other men would take the newcomer to the cave where his horse could be stabled, or to the rope corral in the canyon where it could be taken care of. The bandit would stay a few days, then ride on. It was a strange way of life; nothing else like it has ever been known in America.

One day a full-blooded Cherokee named Jim July hallooed. He was in a bit of a difficulty. Could he stay awhile? Yes, said Belle, who could refuse no one. Jim was a handsome, vigorous man fourteen years younger than herself. And now into this strange household moved Jim July. Belle changed his name to Starr, an act a bit strange in itself. And so they lived—Belle and Pearl and Eddie. The children's new daddy was a horse thief.

Belle was back in business again. And again Belle dressed as a man and became the "brains" of a new band of cattle thieves and outlaws—this woman who had been going steadily downward since Cole had ridden off that day for the North. She was still sending money for his defense. He would soon be out.

One day Pearl told her mother something that shocked Belle: Pearl was going to have a baby. But Pearl would not tell who the father was. And Pearl—the Canadian Lily—gave birth to a child in Siloam Springs, Arkansas, April 22, 1887.

Another shock fell upon hard-pressed Belle. July 14, 1888, her son Eddie was given a prison sentence for horse stealing, and was sent off to the Federal prison in Columbus, Ohio. Immediately Belle got a lawyer and in four months Eddie was pardoned and was back at Younger's Bend. A little good luck at last.

There arrived in the neighborhood one Edgar J. Watson, who had come from Florida to tuck himself away in this wild and remote section. He had been a farmer in Florida, and now rented some land from Belle to work on shares.

The man's wife was lonesome in this new country and struck up an acquaintanceship with Belle. The woman was well educated and, on the whole, was far above the other women in the Bend. The two became friends and saw a great deal of each other. One day Mrs. Watson confided to Belle that her husband had fled from Florida to escape a murder charge. Belle was not too shocked, for she had known many people caught in that awkward situation.

Things went along nicely for a while, then a disagreement sprang up between Belle and Watson over the division of the money from the land. The two had words and there was ill feeling.

The matter was complicated by an incident that happened at the little post office, operated in the crossroads grocery store. By chance a letter addressed to Belle was put in the

W box. Watson got it and opened it. There is no record of what the letter contained, but it was something that Belle did not want him to see. When she found out about it she asked for the letter, but he said he had lost it. She was indignant and, to punish him, entered into a contract with another man to farm her land. Watson promptly hurried to the other man and advised him to break the contract. He said that sheriffs and deputy marshals from Judge Parker's court would be calling on Belle and that he, the new tenant, might be suspected of supporting her in her activities; on top of this, he said, Belle might be sent away to jail again, and no telling who would be boss of the land. He made such a good case of it that the new tenant went to Belle and said he could not go through with their agreement.

At about this time Watson came to call on Belle and the two had hot words. Belle's temper flared up and she said, "I don't suppose the United States officers can make trouble for you, but the Florida officers might."

Watson was shocked. His secret was out. It was evident that Belle was the only one besides his wife who knew this dark and dangerous secret.

If Belle had known a little more about Watson, she would probably have measured her words. Watson, in Florida, had gotten himself into a bit of trouble on the charge of killing his brother-in-law. He had managed to get out of this and had hurried to Arkansas as fast as his heels would take him. No sooner was he there than he was arrested for horse stealing. This also he managed to get out of, but so unpleasant was the situation that he went back to Florida, where he shot two Negroes to death. He got out of this, too, his luck still holding. He got into an argument with a man in Columbia County, Florida, which Watson settled by shooting the man. A mob stormed the jail, determined to have

Watson, but the sheriff beat them off. Watson, with his marvelous luck, got out of this case, too, and settled down in Chatham Bend, south of Chokoloskee Bay, where he became involved in a triple murder. Watson reported he had found the coat of one of the murdered men. The police, becoming suspicious, questioned the glib gentleman, and he got out of this, too! But, all in all, matters were so unpleasant that he skinned out for the Indian Territory where people didn't go around asking foolish questions. And soon he was at Younger's Bend.

And so matters rested for the time being.

Jim July-Starr, who was constantly in and out of trouble, was summoned to go to Fort Smith on a horse-stealing charge, nothing new in the private life of Belle and Jim. Belle, strangely loyal to him, said she would go part way with him as company. The two set out on horseback. They stopped at the King Creek store, on the south side of the South Canadian River, where Belle paid their account of $75. The two rode off together. Jim dark-complexioned and young; Belle in her sidesaddle, the most feared woman in the Indian Territory.

The two parted—Jim to ride on alone to the court of the Hanging Judge, Belle to ride back to Younger's Bend. She stayed overnight with Mrs. Richard Nail on San Bois Creek, twenty miles east of Whitefield, then the next morning rode back to the King Creek store where she bought feed for her horse and ate dinner with the proprietor and his family. She was depressed and gloomy. "Things are not going right."

The proprietor pressed her for an explanation. She sat silent for a moment, then took a silk handkerchief from her pocket, called for a pair of scissors, and cut the handkerchief in two, diagonally. Belle handed half of it to the merchant's wife, and said, "Consider this a keepsake."

Belle spoke of her early days in Missouri and of how terrible the border warfare had seemed. Once she mentioned Cole, then became silent. When she spoke next, it was on another subject.

She left about half-past one. On the way she stopped at the cabin home of Mr. and Mrs. Hyram Barnes to get some sour cornbread that Mrs. Barnes was locally famous for making. When Belle rode up, Watson was in the yard talking to Mr. Barnes; he had a shotgun by his side. As soon as he saw Belle, Watson made an excuse and left. The two did not speak.

Belle, on horseback, ate the sour corn bread, still in the same apprehensive, gloomy mood. She left about half-past three.

At four o'clock "Frog" Hoyt rode his horse off the ferry and started east. He heard the hoofbeats of a running horse and in a moment a riderless horse passed him, leaped into the river, and swam across, going in the direction of Younger's Bend.

Frog Hoyt rode rapidly in the direction the horse had come from; he was not long in finding out what had happened. Belle Starr had been shot off her horse and lay beside the road, dead. Blood was on her face and blood had oozed through her jacket. A large tree stood about thirty steps from where Belle lay. The assailant had hidden himself behind the tree, waited until Belle had passed him, and then had shot her from behind. She had probably not even seen her assassin.

Pearl, twenty years old and now in truth the Canadian Lily, was at home when she, too, heard flying hoofbeats. Looking out the window, she saw her mother's horse. Pearl ran to the stable, saddled a horse, spurred it through the waters of the South Canadian River, and sped down the road. There, her eyes open, vacantly staring at the sky, was the mother who loved Pearl so much.

Pearl got help, and her mother's body was put into a wagon, as were so many bodies in this section and in this day, and went jolting off to the cabin where Belle had lived for ten years, the only true home she had known since she had left Carthage, Missouri.

The women of the neighborhood prepared the body for burial; as they worked, there was the sound of the men digging a grave in the yard. When time for burial came, four Indians went into the living room, picked up the homemade coffin and edged it through the door; each pallbearer had a pistol at his waist; one had hair to his shoulders. All were fierce, rough-looking men, the kind that Belle had associated with so long and whom she had led.

The coffin was placed beside the grave, the lid slid back, and there lay Belle with her arms crossed, bouquet of flowers in one hand, Cole's six-shooter in the other, which, in a way, was an epitome of how she had lived—in many respects a kindly woman, in other respects a cruel, dangerous, vengeful woman. Then, in accordance with the ancient funeral custom of the Cherokees, the Indians filed by the open casket and each tossed into it a piece of corn-meal bread. The lid was nailed down and the coffin lowered. The pallbearers stepped back, and other Indians began to fill the grave, on this her forty-first birthday.

The strange scene was not quite over, for as the last shovelful of dirt was dropped on the grave a man from the rear pushed forward, pointed his rifle at Watson, and said, "I am arresting you for the murder of Belle Starr." The dramatic individual was Jim July-Starr. After Belle and Jim had parted on the road, Jim had gone on to Fort Smith to answer the charge of horse stealing. Pearl had sent him a telegram; he presented this to the court and got permission to return for the funeral. The distance was seventy-five miles and he rode it as fast as he could, arriving while the funeral was being held.

"If you kill me you'll kill the wrong man," said Watson calmly.

Jim was taken back by the offhand way Watson treated his threat, and lowered his rifle.

Jim had no warrant, but he did have the right to demand an arrest and to take the person to the proper authorities. The next day a strange procession set out for Fort Smith—Watson on horseback with his wrists bound, Jim July-Starr with his trusty rifle across his saddle, and a Cherokee police officer.

Watson was given a hearing before a commissioner in the United States Federal Court, but Jim had not brought witnesses. He was given two weeks to get evidence, but was not able to find any. On top of this, Jim's reputation was far from lily white; no one wanted to get mixed up with anything that he had to do with, and so, for lack of evidence, the case fell to pieces and was not brought before the grand jury.

The cool and collected Watson stayed at Younger's Bend for a while, then moved to Arkansas and in no time was up on a charge of horse stealing. He got out of this, too, as he seemed to get out of everything. Matters in Florida having cooled off, he returned, no great boon for Florida. We'll see, in a moment, what happened to him in the state that spawned him.

Belle had a strange trait of character—she was always loyal to her current husband. In turn she was loyal to Jim Reed, to Blue Duck, and to Jim July-Starr. But the one she loved was Cole. Her loyalty to Jim July-Starr is brought out in her oral will which is to be found in Cherokee records, Vol. 11, page 15:

Personally appeared before me, M. Kraft and Charles Acton who state on oath that they heard Belle Starr say on several occasions, a short time before her death and while in sound mind, that if anything should happen or befall her, or that she should die, that the improvement on which she was living would be James L. Starr's. The improvement is situated on the Canadian River in the Cherokee Nation.

M. Kraft
Charles Acton

Sworn and subscribed to before me
this 25th day of February, 1889.

H. J. Vann, Clerk,
Canadian District,
Cherokee Nation.

Belle lay undisturbed for some time in the yard of her home, and then, during a period when the family was away, someone dug open the grave, pried up the lid to the coffin, and took Cole Younger's pistol.

Here's a word or two about what happened later to cold-blooded Watson. The word is from Charles Sherod Smallwood, usually known as "Ted" Smallwood. He was postmaster of Chokoloskee, Florida, until 1941, when he retired in favor of his daughter Thelma, who is now the postmistress. The town is on an island near Everglades, Florida, and not too far from the Tamiami Trail. The material was supplied to me by Charlton W. Tebeau, of the University of Miami, and appears in *The Chokoloskee Bay Country, With Reminiscences by C. S. "Ted" Smallwood,* Copeland Studies in Florida History, 1955 edition.

Said Ted Smallwood:

Ed Watson, of Chatham Bend, was always gettin' himself into trouble, him bein' that kind. Durin' his lifetime he had three wives, all Columbia County women. He got into trouble here over a matter of shooting, and dusted out for Arkansas, then moved into Indian Territory, where he was a neighbor of Belle Starr. He promptly had trouble with her, which he ended by killing her. He got out of this an' headed back for Florida. On the way, as he was comin' through Arcadia, he killed Quinn Bass in a nasty shooting scrape. He got out of that too, and for a while made a living cuttin' buttonwood and running it to Key West. Then he got into trouble with Adolphus Santini, one of our best citizens. It ended by him cutting Santini's throat who had a livid scar the rest of his life. It cost Watson $200 to get out of that scrape, life bein' rather simple here in our Everglades section. Watson bought a claim on Lostman's Key from Winky Atwell. But before Watson could get on it, a man named Tucker got on it and his nephew and they wouldn't get off. It ended up by Watson killing Tucker and the nephew, and that cost him plenty. Then Watson killed a man named Tolens. This scrape cost him a lot of money. Watson came back to Chatham Bend and began makin' syrup, but was soon in trouble again. He killed Dutchy Melvin. In fact, one way or another, Watson was accused of killing, or participatin' in the killing, of seven men. One day he came to my place and said he was goin' to kill Leslie Cox, him becoming increasingly bold. He went to the mouth of the River and a few days later came back and Cox was dead. People had got aroused over Watson's wild ways. A crowd gathered at my landing and I knew that trouble was in the offing. Watson's wife was with my wife, and we all felt apprehensive. I could hear his boat coming down the pass an' I didn't want any of it, the situation bein' what it was. Armed men were waiting. To make a long story short, I heard shooting and after a spell I went down to the landing and Watson was lyin' there, dead as you please. This was in October, 1910. They carried him to Rabbit Key and buried him. Some time later his body was dug up and taken to Fort Myers where it was re-buried. That was the end of the man who killed Belle Starr, the bandit and outlaw woman of Arkansas and the Indian Territory."

Croy's Check-up: I wrote to William R. Spear, editor of the *Fort Myers News-Press,* to see how the above statements meshed with his information. This is his answer:

Edgar J. Watson was shot and killed on the boat landing at the store of the late Ted Smallwood, at Chokoloskee, October 24, 1910. He is buried in a family plot in Fort Myers Cemetery. The plot is marked by a large slab which says just WATSON. His particular grave in the plot is marked by a smaller stone which says

Edgar J. Watson

Nov. 11, 1855

Oct. 24, 1910

Watson was first buried at Rabbit Key, just as you state. His body was subsequently taken up and brought to Fort Myers for burial by the late Captain William B. Collier of Marco.

And so ends the story of the man who killed Belle Starr.

CHAPTER XIV

The Great Day Comes—Cole Is
Released from Prison in Minnesota.
Now He Can Take Up His Job
of Selling Tombstones

COLE's entrance record gets right down to business:

> Sentenced November 20, 1876, to life
> imprisonment for bank robbery and the
> murder of Mr. Heywood, cashier of the
> Northfield bank at the time of the
> robbery—
> Prison number—699
> Age—32 years
> Height—5 feet, 11½ inches
> Weight—230 pounds
> Occupation—farmer
> Native—Missouri State

Only one building of what is known as "the old prison"
still stands, and this is now, of all things, a condensed-milk
storage plant. The other buildings were pulled down in 1936
to riprap the Mississippi River. And here into "the old
prison" Cole was popped, to the excitement of the prisoners,
for, except for Jesse and Frank James, he was the most
famous bandit in America. After the fashion of the day at
this prison, his name was painted on his cell door, as if this

158

were to be his permanent home. Well, Cole didn't intend for it to be that at all. Even before he had crossed its threshold, he was planning to quit it. It will be recalled, when he was put in the spring wagon and started on the way to Madelia, that he asked, "Did Frank and Jesse get away?" By the time he was on the train he had thought it over and, when asked the names of the two men who had escaped, said they were Howard and Woods. He said they had just joined and that he didn't know much about them. When first questioned he had said that the reason they had robbed the Minnesota bank was because crooked gamblers had fleeced them. This was hardly an inspiration, as Cole soon realized, and he began to tell how badly General Butler had treated Southerners. That was much better. When he was up against a situation, no one could look quite as injured and misunderstood as Cole. In a way, he was an actor and he was good at the job.

Yes, he was going to get out. He had never been in prison in his life, and he had never been captured during guerrilla days, and now he made up his mind that he was going to use every device, every expedient to make himself a free man. Then back to Missouri.

The beginning was not brilliant. He was put to work making washtubs. Cole was considered so desperate that a special guard was put over him with instructions to shoot if he made a false move. A false move was about the last thing in the world that Cole intended to make; he was going to be a model prisoner and get a pardon.

The popping of Cole into prison had been thrilling news. How could the son of a self-respecting family become a mad dog? What kind of mentality did he have? And so reporters came, a bit surprised to find a dignified man who talked grammatically and was mild of manner, the kind of man children like to call uncle.

Representatives from women's clubs came to see him; mostly they wanted to ask if he didn't wish he had led a different life. Cole, always polite, told the ladies sadly that he wished he had. It seemed to give them an immense amount of satisfaction.

One of the organizations that sent a representative to probe Cole was the St. Paul chapter of the Phrenological Society. America at this time was much interested in reading character from "the configurations of the human head." The mastermind of this group was Orson Fowler, of New York, who had invented a chart that showed from bumps just how the human mind worked. Mankind had puzzled over this matter for generations, but Orson Fowler, by a lucky stroke, had solved it. He had a chart drawn of the human head and laid off into sections, thirty-three in number. If you had a bump in twelve, that was entirely different from sprouting one in thirteeen. People believed so implicitly in this happy solution of the problem of human behavior that in New York employers made job applicants go to Orson Fowler to have their heads read before they would be given jobs. And so off to the prison went Professor George Morris of St. Paul to plumb Cole's soul. The mystified Cole was brought out, seated in a chair in the warden's office, and the professor opened his little bag. He took a tape measure, and solemnly measured Cole's head, fore and aft, and jotted down his findings. Then he took a pair of calipers and measured the bumps on Cole's head, carefully setting down his discoveries. Then he put a *papier-mâché* mask over Cole's head and fitted it to the skull as carefully as a jeweler adjusting the hairspring of a lady's watch. After he had gone over

Cole thoroughly, he thanked him, and Cole was led back to his cell, not knowing that his secrets had been laid bare.

This is what Professor Morris reported:

> His head measures 23 and three-fourths inches in circumference by 14½ inches over Veneration.
> Intellect—good, practical
> Comparativeness—6
> Amativeness—4
> Destinativeness—6½
> Secretiveness—5
> Spirituality and hope—5
> Vitativeness—14
> Alimentativeness—8
> Confugality—4
> Human nature—6½
> Temperaments—all 6
> Conclusion: The subject is a national leader; if he had been in the North and educated at West Point, he would have been as useful a man as General Sheridan, or General Hancock.

Meantime, Cole was back in his cell, never suspecting that if he had gone to West Point his career would have been vastly different.

One of his problems was his brother Jim, part of whose jaw had been shot away. The prison doctor, Dr. T. C. Clarke, undertook to remove a bullet which had been lodged in Jim's head, near the brain. It was a delicate operation and was a successful one, but Jim continued to suffer from his jaw wound. He became more and more moody; to escape reality he began to read socialistic literature and became, in prison words, a "radical."

Cole was promoted from tubs to the library, and here he

received visitors. It was a large, well-lighted room, with a bay window that looked across the prison yard. In the room were two cages of singing canaries. Cole fed and took care of the birds, talking to them as if they were children. On the walls were autographed pictures of some rather well-known people. Ladies sent him flowers. Much of the time that he sat in the library, serving as librarian, he wore a straw hat. He was growing bald and believed the hat protected him from drafts. When a lady visitor entered, he politely removed his hat; when she left, he put it back on again.

After a time Cole was moved to the prison hospital. He had nursed men during his guerrilla days, now he was back to that again. But he liked it and he made a good nurse. Once, during this part of his prison career, he said, "I hate to see men die."

The monotonous days went by, one about like another. But now and then something outstanding happened. April 4, 1882, a guard appeared at Cole's cell and said that the warden wanted to see Cole in his office. Many times this had happened; sometimes he had been called for important visitors, a few times it had been to see bushwhackers he had ridden with in the old days. Today a reporter was waiting. Cole expected it to be a routine interview—a reporter trying to "work up" a story.

"I have news for you, Cole," said the reporter. "Jesse James has been killed."

His old friend-enemy—killed.

"How?" Cole managed to ask.

The reporter told briefly what had happened. "What have you to say?"

Cole was in a spot; he must not let himself be tied in with Jesse.

"It comes in the nature of a surprise," he said when he

had collected himself. "I have no sympathy for men engaged in the kind of things he is reported to have been in. It will be easy to identify him. He had a scar in his upper right lung, left from the Civil War."

"Did you know him well?"

"No, I did not know him well. I knew him during the latter part of the Civil War. We did not get along well together. I was never in sympathy with what he was doing."

"Was he in the Northfield raid?"

Cole had been asked that question a thousand times. "There were two men in it—Howard and Woods—who were never captured. I knew no men identifying themselves as the James brothers."

At last the reporter let the matter drop and Cole was led back to his cell, having revealed nothing at all.

And this attitude Cole preserved wholly and completely. The James boys had not been in the raid; the two who had escaped were men who never revealed anything about themselves. That pardon! Cole was determined to get it.

In 1882 something happened in Cole's favor that he knew nothing about; it had to do with the Battle of Lone Jack. Alert readers will remember how Cole saved the life of a young Confederate soldier—the young chap was about to ride into a nest of Union soldiers when Cole stopped him on the road and warned him. The young man was Warren Carter Bronaugh. The event on the highway had made a deep impression on the young man, but he had never known the name of the handsome, nice-mannered young guerrilla who saved him. One day in reading about the capture of the Younger brothers in Minnesota, Bronaugh saw Cole's picture. He looked at it long and hard. Why! This was the man who had saved his life fourteen years ago. A deep and burning desire came over Bronaugh to do something for Cole. He would not rest until he freed him from prison—an ambitious urge, indeed. Bronaugh was now a farmer near Clinton, Missouri, without much money, only a feeling of deep obligation to Cole. He made a covenant with himself that he would get Cole out. The first thing, he decided, was to go to the prison and make sure that the captured man was his benefactor. And there he went—of all times—on his honeymoon, for he could not afford to make two trips. The warden looked him over sourly. Coming to Minnesota to get the murderers out of prison. But Bronaugh presented his case so fervently that the warden, A. J. Reed, was won over. Finally he called a guard and said, "Take this man to see the Youngers, but make him bare his sleeve to his elbow and you stand close enough to hear every word that is said."

Bronaugh was led down the clanking corridor to a cell inside which stood a man.

"Are you Cole Younger?"

"That is my name."

Bronaugh thrust his bared arm through the bars. "I want to shake your hand."

The two men shook hands.

"Look at me and see if you remember me," said Bronaugh.

Cole's gray eyes peered through the bars. "So far as I know, sir, I have never seen you before in my life."

"Does the name Chapel Hill Road, near Lone Jack, Missouri, mean anything to you?"

"It does, sir, for I was there," said the always-polite Cole.

"Do you remember a young man from Colonel Vard Cockrell's company coming up on horseback and do you remember directing him not to continue in the direction he was going?"

Cole studied for a moment. "I remember it vaguely, sir."

"I'm the young man and you saved my life!" cried Bronaugh. "I would not be here this minute if you had not done what you did that day at Lone Jack."

"I'm glad I could be of service," said Cole respectfully.

"I want to show my appreciation by getting you out of prison."

"Oh!" said Cole. "I would like to get out of prison. I would like that the best of anything in the world."

"I will get you out!" cried the young crusader.

As Bronaugh left he passed a guard in the corridor with a corrugated iron pail. The man handed the pail through an opening in the bars of one of the cells. The pail contained gruel for Jim Younger, who could not eat solid food.

Bronaugh extended his bare arm through the bars and talked to Jim, assuring him, as he had Cole, that he would free him.

Cole was pleased to have anything that broke the monotony of prison life, and did not take too seriously what the other had said. But he did not know the fervor that consumed Bronaugh.

Bronaugh went back to St. Paul with his bride and began to "sound out" opinion in Minnesota. For two days he went among the people—on the streets and in hotel lobbies—asking if they would favor the release of the Younger brothers. One man looked at him and said, "You are a fool in this state even to propose it."

Bronaugh returned to Missouri and immediately set about trying to get Cole out—Cole, the most dangerous, the most infamous prisoner in the United States. Get him out! Well, he would, said the young zealot. He began traveling over Missouri, seeing important and influential people, telling over and over the tale of how the Youngers were the victims of the Border War and saying that they were really good men at heart. He might as well have told it to a hurricane. No one would listen seriously. But he kept on. He owed Cole Younger his life; he was going to get Cole out somehow.

At about this time there was a drive to start a weekly prison paper. The idea was fine, but there was a catch: the convicts had to do it with their own money. Two hundred dollars was needed. Cole, with his two brothers, contributed $50 and on August 10, 1887, the *Prison Mirror* was launched —the first prison paper in the United States. It is still running. The paper interviewed me and turned out a nice article with touches of humor here and there.

February 5, 1889, was another important day. Word again was brought to Cole that he was wanted in the warden's office, and Cole started on the trip he had come to know so well. It would be a reporter, he thought. And it was. But this time the reporter had startling news: Belle Starr had been killed.

The reporter told briefly the details. "I would like to have your comment. The dispatch says she was your wife. This is the way it reads: 'She is said to have married Cole Younger at the close of the Civil War, but left him and married a desperado named Sam Starr. Belle Starr had the reputation of being the most desperate woman on the border. The woman left a daughter named Pearl Younger.'"

Cole looked at the warden he was so anxious to please, then spoke more for him than for the newspaper reporter:

"In reply I will say that I was never married in my life. I cannot say that I ever knew the woman Belle Starr. In 1869, at Scyene, Dallas County, Texas, I did know a young woman named Belle Shirley. She eloped with a man named Reed and the couple went to California. They returned in 1872. Reed was killed in a brawl of some kind. I remember the woman as being vivacious, full of life, vigor, and daring, especially as to horseback riding, and she was an accomplished pianist. In fact, she was a sort of madcap. Still, there was nothing bad about the woman in the general acceptance of the term. Her parents in Scyene were very respectable people. The only explanation I can think of as connecting my name with this woman is that she lived at Younger's Bend, in the Indian Territory, named after some member of our family. But you may say positively and emphatically that the woman killed was not Cole Younger's wife, because he was never blessed with one."

"Have you any other comment, Mr. Younger?"

"Yes. Have you noticed that there has been a play running in St. Paul and Minneapolis representing border scenes?"

"Yes. And you have been a prominent character in the plot," answered the reporter.

"That is my point. I believe that this whole thing has been gotten up to advertise the show. Looks very much like it, indeed."

The ordeal was over, and Cole was led back, wondering, no doubt, if he had prejudiced his pardon chances.

A few months after this Cole suffered another blow. It had to do with Bob Younger. Bob was quiet, soft-spoken, and known as the library's best customer. In the great man hunt he had been shot through the lung and now began to waste away from tuberculosis. Cole helped to wait on him in the prison hospital and sat for hours at his bedside. When it was seen that the end was close, sister Retta was sent for. Monday evening, September 16, 1889, Bob indicated that he wanted to speak to her and Cole. The two bent over him, but his voice was too weak. The funeral was held in the prison chapel. The body was taken to Lee's Summit and buried in the family plot. He lacked a few weeks of being thirty-six.

Meantime Bronaugh was working diligently on his seemingly crazy project. He went to the governor of Missouri, who told him the matter could never be accomplished and that he himself would help in no way. Bronaugh turned his attention to the members of the Missouri State Legislature, and to the state senators. Politics entered; the men said they would do nothing to help get a murderer and outlaw out of prison. Bronaugh put a mortgage on his home. Money! He would have to have money for letters and telegrams and for travel, and so he began to take money from those who sympathized with his helpless cause. One of those who had sent money was Belle Starr.

Nothing discouraged Bronaugh. He wrote thousands of letters; he had a grip that he called his "Cole Younger Bag" and he would take it into an office and set it down on the floor beside him and extract letters and testimonials.

Bronaugh went to a Baptist minister in Kansas City and got from him a letter of introduction to George A. Pillsbury, the flour manufacturer, who was the richest man in Minnesota. The minister in Kansas City had been Pillsbury's pastor. Pillsbury was giving to the Baptist Church $20,000 each year for foreign missionary work. Bronaugh went to Pillsbury's office and set his bag down.

Pillsbury looked at him belligerently. "What, exactly, do you want?"

"I want you, if you will, to write a letter to the governor of Minnesota recommending a pardon for the Youngers."

"Me write a letter recommending a pardon!" thundered the great man. "Why, I would head a mob to hang them! Never, never will I lend my aid to free them."

Bronaugh went to Major Emory Stallsworth Foster, whose life Cole had saved. Major Foster wrote the Board of Pardons, detailing what had happened that bloody day at the Battle of Lone Jack. The Board of Pardons did not answer the letter. Cole was guilty and must suffer.

Readers will remember young Stephen Elkins, Cole's schoolteacher. Cole had save his life at the Battle of Lone Jack when Quantrill's men were upon him. Cole's old teacher was now United States Senator Stephen B. Elkins, from West Virginia. He sent Bronaugh $100 and wrote the Board of Pardons, telling what Cole had done for him so long ago. His letter was not answered.

By this time not only was Minnesota aroused but, to some degree, the whole nation. Every detail of the lives of the Youngers was being examined. The boys had come from a good family; they were, many said, the victims of their times. And then, just as the situation was beginning to look favorable, a most dreadful blow fell on Bronaugh's cause. A paper dug up the absurd story from the Appler book recounting how Cole had lined up fifteen captured Union prisoners and had killed them to see how many men the Enfield rifle would shoot through—in this state where all the soldiers were Union men. There was not one word of truth in the story; in fact, Cole had not even been there. But the papers took it up and people wrote in to the Board of Pardons. Cole protested, but his protests did no good. He had barbarously slaughtered the fifteen men and that was the end of it.

Cole was so alarmed by the evil this story was doing him that on August 1, 1886, he wrote Governor William R. Marshall of Minnesota: "I understand there are several so-called histories of the James and Younger brothers, but I had nothing to do with them. I never gave an interview to anyone getting up such a history. I have steadily refused all application for such information."

Bronaugh went to the governor of Minnesota, asking him

if he would recommend a pardon. The governor said that it would be political suicide for him to do so.

The hardships, rebuffs, and indignities that Bronaugh suffered are almost incredible. He became poorer and poorer; his family suffered. He was forced to become manager of the Confederate Home in Missouri. At night he sat at his desk writing letters to important people; not only that, but at his own expense he went to see the people and talked to them in person.

An agreement was reached that no candidate could run for nomination for governor of Minnesota who advocated freeing the Youngers. Even this did not defeat the indomitable man.

He had a triumph. He went to B. G. Yates, who was the posse member who had shot Jim Younger through the jaw, and got Yates to say he would like to see the Youngers pardoned. Yates wrote the governor: "I would rather have a pardon from Your Excellency in my hand and take it to the Youngers than to have a present of $1,000."

Denman Thompson was appearing in *The Old Homestead*, a tremendously successful play of the back-home type. Bronaugh went to Thompson and told the story of the Youngers. Denman Thompson was so impressed by Bronaugh's sincerity and earnestness that he gave Bronaugh $100 to help free the Youngers.

Ignatius Donnelly was congressman from Minnesota. He had written a book "proving" that Francis Bacon had written Shakespeare. The book had created a sensation and the brilliant, erratic Donnelly was one of the prominent men in the United States. Bronaugh went to him and told his story. Ignatius Donnelly promptly came out saying that the Youngers should be freed.

It was announced that a meeting of the Board of Pardons

was to be held in Governor Clough's office in St. Paul, July 8, 1897. Immediately the state was aroused. Farmers came in their wagons to protest again the freeing of the Youngers. Northfield sent a delegation crying for vengeance.

When the meeting was called to order, the mayor of Faribault, A. D. Keyes, rose and said, "There are three things we want to know. Cole Younger can tell us.

"First: Was Frank James in the bank?

"Second: Who was the last man to leave the bank?

"Third: Who rode the dun horse?

"We claim it is not too much for the Youngers to remain where they are until they disclose the name of the man who killed Heywood. It is not an element of good citizenship to conceal a murderer. If the Youngers are the good citizens they claim to be, they will go on the stand and, by telling the truth, assist the authorities of this state to bring the Northfield murderer to justice. If the murderer was Frank James, as we are led to believe, then he has never suffered for his crime and should be brought back to Minnesota and punished."

When this was told to Cole in prison, he became agitated. If he would tell who had killed the cashier he might advance his cause. But he had always been loyal to Frank James—he would continue to be. "The man who killed the cashier was one of the men who rode with us under the names of Howard and Woods," he said, and that was all he would say.

Affidavits of eyewitnesses were presented at the meeting; all charged that Cole had killed the young Swede.

At last the meeting was over. Instead of having helped the cause of the Youngers, it had harmed it.

One day a bit of good luck came Bronaugh's way. The governor of Minnesota (who had been born in Missouri) said he was coming to Missouri and that he would discuss the matter with the governor of Missouri. When the time came, Bronaugh sat with the two governors and did all he could to bring about action.

The indomitable Bronaugh struggled on, never ceasing, never stopping. People who had at first bitterly opposed him now began to think that the Youngers had been punished enough; and, too, there was a better understanding of both the hates the Border War had aroused and that people are often molded by giant forces they don't even understand. On top of this, the Youngers had been model prisoners for twenty-five years. And so, finally, the Board of Parole agreed to free the prisoners on a conditional pardon. But not wholly, for there was a stout string tied to the pardon: neither of the Youngers was to leave the state of Minnesota. In addition, Cole was not to "exhibit himself in any dime museum, circus, theater, opera house, or any other place of public amusement, or assembly, where a charge is made for admission. He shall on the twentieth day of each month write the warden of the state prison a report of himself.... He shall in all respects conduct himself honestly ... and abstain from the use of intoxicating liquors." As Cole had never drunk, the last stipulation was not too much of a problem.

And now, before he was to be released, Cole got a job in an unexpected quarter—selling tombstones. That there was an element of humor attached to this no one at the time seems to have noticed. Certainly not Cole, for his sense of humor was not a lively one. He was, in fact, becoming more and more pontifical. He could no longer utter a simple "yes"; instead, he would say, "I am inclined to think I would answer affirmatively on the matter."

Bronaugh raced to St. Paul, where he went to the same hotel he had gone to on his honeymoon nineteen years before. During the time in between he had gone into debt and

had impoverished himself to bring about the matter he believed in so deeply and sincerely.

Cole's position in the prison had changed. He had been
promoted to head nurse in the hospital. On this morning he
was in the hospital when one of the guards came and told
him he was wanted "down front." Then the guard went to
Jim, who worked in the library, and told him he, too, was
wanted "down front." Joyous news.

A deputy warden came in and said, "On the way, stop in
and put on a civilian suit."

The two men went into the chief warden's office. "And
now," said the chief warden, "here is a grip for each of you."
He gave each of them a canvas valise.

Cole was fifty-seven years old and was almost bald. He
had grown portly and over him was a prison pallor.

When Cole came out, Bronaugh, who was waiting at the
door, leaped forward. "I said I would be the first Missourian
to shake hands with you, Cole, and I want to do it. I've
waited nineteen years for this."

The two men shook hands and now, after the first greet-
ing, stood a little embarrased, ill at ease, and half-silent.

"How's everything back in Jackson County?" asked Cole.

"Just fine, Cole. Just fine."

Again there was a little silence.

"Did you send any telegrams to Missouri?" asked Cole.

"I sent lots of 'em and not one to anybody who is not
your friend."

"I am so happy I want to give you a Methodist handshake,
Bronaugh," said Cole, losing a little of his bishop bearing.
"Y'know, when a Methodist feels good he wants to shake
hands. I feel like shaking hands with the whole world."

He gave Bronaugh a Methodist handshake.

Turning to the reporters, Cole said, "Y'know, Bronaugh

is a Methodist—a regular ol' handshaker himself. Shake hands again, Bronaugh."

The two shook hands.

"As I stand here," continued Cole, "I haven't got a grudge against anybody in the world. It's a wonderful feeling, Bronaugh."

"I know it must be," said the half-weeping Bronaugh.

"Let me shake your hand again, Bronaugh," said Cole, for lack of something better to say and do.

The two shook hands again.

"It's great to be out," said Cole.

"I know it must be," said Bronaugh.

"It certainly is," repeated Cole.

"Do you suppose they know about it in St. Paul?" asked Cole.

"They've got an extra on the street."

"Oh!" said Cole, visibly pleased. "Do you suppose they know it in Jackson County?"

The modern Rip Van Winkle started to walk down the street in Stillwater, and with him went the men to see him in his new world.

When Jim Younger walked out with Cole, a free man, he did not have the zest that Cole had. He walked along silent, for the most part, making no comment and talking to none of the people who walked with the two men to see what their reactions would be. He had been offered a job, but took little interest even in this.

The party arrived at a cigar store. "I feel like setting you up," said Cole, and the party went in. The clerk started to wait on them perfunctorily, then blinked. "Ain't this Cole Younger?"

"Your surmise is correct," said the once more formal Cole.

"Well," gaped the clerk, "the treat's on me."

The party, after lighting up, started on down the street, smoke clouds wafting after them.

One of the reporters said, "I want to take you into this store." When the party went in, the reporter showed Cole a queer-looking contraption fastened to the wall. "I can talk to my paper in St. Paul through this," he said.

"Can you really?" was all the astonished man could say.

Out on the street again there was a chugging and a groaning, and an odd-looking vehicle thudded past. "That's a horseless carriage," explained the reporter. "It's from St. Paul."

Cole stared in astonishment. "I think a horse would be safer," he said.

The reporters, who were enjoying themselves, took Cole into another store where the proprietor played a phonograph. Cole gazed at it in unbelief; finally, convinced, he said, "Just think of a machine that can talk and sing."

Warden Wolfer, who was enjoying watching Cole basking in his new-found freedom, said that he would take Cole and Jim on what was called a "naphtha launch" trip on Lake St. Croix. As Cole got into the boat he stood for a moment looking across the lake. "This is the most wonderful day of my life," he said.

It was a new and astonishing world—a fabulously enriched world—a world of comforts and conveniences and luxuries that Cole had never dreamed of when the doors had closed behind him.

At last the great day was over and Cole and Jim—in their new clothes and their new hopes—went to a hotel in Stillwater and stayed overnight. Now they would have to undertake their jobs and become useful citizens. But the two could not leave the state of Minnesota. Cole wanted to get back to Missouri. He would find some way to do it.

The second day Cole was free, Dr. M. E. Withrow invited Cole to have dinner with him at his mother's farm a short distance from Stillwater. Dr. Withrow was the resident surgeon at the prison and the two had worked together in the hospital. As they were driving along in a horse and buggy, Cole said, "Please stop a minute, Doctor."

Dr. Withrow drew up and looked about him, but did not see anything of special interest.

Cole sat silent for some moments looking out across the landscape. "You can go on now, Doctor. This is the first time in twenty-five years that I have seen the sun set. I never knew before how beautiful a sunset was."

In Kansas City, Missouri, Jesse James, Junior, was behind the counter in his cigar store when a friend, T. T. Crittenden, Junior, came in and said, "Jess, I've got news for you. Cole and Jim have been paroled in Minnesota."

Jesse, Junior, looked surprised, then said, "Is that so? I'm glad of it. I think twenty-five years in prison has been long enough for them to suffer."

CHAPTER XV

Cole Returns to Missouri. Opens in a Wild West Show. The Old Outlaw Dies Five Miles from Where He Was Born

Cole and Jim were each to receive $60 a month. If there was an element of humor in peddling tombstones, they made no mention of it. And so now each got into a buggy and started out over the state. It was something new for the two to ride in a buggy; horseback, yes, but not in a slow-rolling, one-horse buggy. They stopped at farmhouses, showed pictures, and talked up their wares. The farmers were delighted to have such distinguished callers and asked them to stay for dinner, but this—as Cole put it—didn't sell stones.

Things did not go too well. One day, as Jim was getting out of his buggy, the horse lunged forward and Jim was knocked down and injured. He was confined to bed for three weeks, and, discouraged, gave up trying to sell tombstones and got a job writing life insurance. He had been at this about a month when his company found that he, a convict on conditional parole, could not draw up a legal contract. He was depressed and began to sit in his hotel, brooding.

Cole himself was not doing too well. August 31, 1901, from Wadena, Cole wrote Warden Wolfer:

"I'm not selling as many stones as I would like to. This

is a new country and takes no interest in the gravestones of its people, mostly newcomers. The people need their ready money to improve their homes, and so leave their dead to wait. Some of my days are 18 hrs long, but I don't care for that, if I can sell the stones."

At last Cole gave it up and got a job—of all things—in the police department, in St. Paul, under Chief John J. O'Connor. Now Cole was against all rascals, and ready to pop them into prison.

Each month Number 699 had to turn in a report to the warden. I looked over some of them and plucked out one as a sample, dated January 30, 1903:

Question: By whom have you been employed the last month?
Answer: By the Honorable J. J. O'Connor, St. Paul, Minn.
Q: At what kind of work?
A: I have had grip & rheumatism.
Q: How many days have you worked?
A: 0.
Q: What has been your wages per day, or month?
A: 0.
Q: How much cash have you on hand?
A: $50.
Q: Give total earnings for the month.
A: A friend sent me $100.
Q: What have been your expenditures?
A: Board 0. Clothes $25. Incidentals $5.
Q: If you have been idle during any portion of the month state why.
A: I have been doctoring for gravel & the grippe.
Q: Where do you spend your evenings?
A: At home, 551 State Street, St. P.
Q: Do you attend church?
A: Yes. Once.

Q: Do you use tobacco?

A: Yes.

Q: Do you use intoxicating liquors?

A: No.

Q: State what you read.

A: Magazines & daily papers.

Q: Have you attended any public meeting, dances, picnics or parties?

A: I attended the organization of the Legislature in both houses, and Preachers meeting.

Q: What are your prospects?

A: Bright.

His prospects were not quite so rosy as he set them down, as we shall see.

As for Jim, things had not gone well since his accident. He began to avoid his friends; when visitors came to his hotel, the Reardon, in St. Paul, he would send down word by the bellboy that he was "indisposed." The crisis came Sunday afternoon, October 19, 1901. Placing a pistol to his head, just over his right ear, he killed himself. His body was taken back to Missouri where it was buried in the family plot beside Bob's. The two brothers had "gone home."

Meantime, Bronaugh had not ceased his labors to get an unconditional pardon for Cole, and this the amazing man did, in February, 1903—twenty years after he had determined to show his appreciation for Cole's saving his life. And now the Board of Pardons reversed itself and told Cole to get out of the state and never come back. Cole's heart must have sung a little private song. Now he was a free man; he could go anywhere in the United States he wanted to, except, of course, Minnesota.

And now, as the very hour approached, he began to wonder how he would be received in his home state. He had brought disgrace to it. Missouri was called the "Mother of Bandits," and that was a true statement, for it had produced more outlaws than any other state in the Union. And now, he, a leader, was returning.

About eleven o'clock at night, February 16, 1903, a large, florid-looking man carrying a canvas bag got off the Kansas City train at Lee's Summit and looked at the darkened streets. Was it possible that it was forty-two years since he had "taken to the brush" from this very town? He was young, then, and was moved by a great passion—his belief that the South was right. And now he was an old man; his cause had lost and he had lost. Now that he was back, how would he make a living? He had no trade or occupation; he had been a soldier, an outlaw, a prisoner all his life. Also important was how would the "home folks" receive him? He had disgraced his family, he had disgraced the town. Would his old friends turn against him? He went down the street, entered the hotel, and looked self-consciously around. The lobby was filled with smoking and tobacco-chewing men who paid no attention to him.

He went to the desk, and set his grip down and said in a low voice, "Have you got a room?"

"Yes." The clerk pushed a book toward him. "Please register."

Cole signed "T. C. Younger."

The clerk looked at the register. "What address?"

Cole turned the book around and wrote, "Lee's Summit, Missouri."

The clerk started to write the number of the room, then glanced at the name and looked very hard. "Are you Cole Younger?"

"Yes."

"Oh!" He studied Cole for an agonizing moment, "You've just got back to town, then?"

"Yes."

There was an awkward silence. "I'll show you your room."

Cole followed in the wake of the unresponsive young man. "I've heard a good deal about you."

The word spread that the famous—or infamous—Cole Younger had "come home." A few people dropped in to see him. Cole was ill at ease, and said as little as he could, meanwhile watching the people carefully.

He got Todd M. George, who is still living and who told me about it, to hire a horse and buggy for him, and the two drove out to the old farmhouse where Cole had been born so long ago. Then he had the boy drive him over the old trails that Cole had ridden, and to some of the spots where he had hidden. He made only one remark that Mr. George can remember. "Everything was so different then," he said.

Cole was morose for some days, hurrying through the lobby, speaking to hardly anyone. Little by little the townsfolk began to feel more kindly toward him. After all, he had come from a good family; he had come from the most bloody county in the Civil War; he had been swept up by the times. Almost every family in the county had had some member who had killed or robbed; and Cole had been little different from their own sons and fathers.

Cole, now that he was being "accepted," felt better. The people spoke of the Northfield raid and his days in prison and tried to lead him into talk about this, but he would say nothing.

In a few days Frank James came—still tall and thin, bony-nosed and stoop-shouldered. A much heavier Cole Younger shook hands with him, and as they did so they called each other Buck and Bud, names they had used in the old guerrilla days. The two went for a walk beyond alien ears—these two who had killed so many men during the Border War and during their "riding days"—as outlawry in Missouri was delicately described. How much had happened since the Madelia swamps: Belle Starr was dead, Jesse had been killed by an assassin, Arch Clements (who'd led the Liberty bank raid) was dead, Tucker Bassham was dead, and Hobbs Kerry, the none-too-bright, was dead and safely buried. And so was Bill Ryan, who had gone on the monstrous drunk. Dick Liddil was as dead as a doornail, and so was George Shepherd, who had slept that night in bed with Cole. And Bob Ford and Charlie Ford (no great loss, here), Wood Hite and Clarence Hite (Frank's cousins), Andy McGuire, Art McCoy—they had all gone. Only Frank James and Cole and Jim Cummins were left, and Jim Cummins was small potatoes. No one in the band had ever had any use for the little sniveler and cry-baby. Jesse's widow had died, too, leaving two children—Jesse, Junior, and Mary. Frank's mother still lived and so did Frank's wife. But most of the men and women who knew old-time days and ways were gone.

Not one of the great post-Civil War outlaws was left—the bold men who had entered a bank and taken their chances with a posse—men who, by their skill and craft and daring, either lived or died. Banks were still being robbed and now and then a train was held up, but now the bandit existed only a short time; with luck he might rob twice and then he was dead or in prison. Jesse James had ridden and robbed fourteen and a half years. Cole had been at it ten years before he had been cut down. The new bandit was really not a bandit at all.

The next day more people came to see Cole. He sat in a chair in the lobby, smoking a meerschaum. The men he reached out his hand to; when a lady came up, he got to his feet and removed his big black hat. "Pleased, ma'am," he said. If he knew her he called her by name, delighted he could do so. Sometimes he said, "I reckon this is the first time we ever met, but I've known your family a long time, a credit to the county." (He was especially addicted to the use of "reckon.")

He moved into the house of his niece Miss Nora Hall and her brother Harry Younger Hall.

How did he spend his time after he got back? He visited his old friends, for he was a sociable creature, and, although he wouldn't admit it, he liked the attention people paid him. An example of what he did after his return was told to me by H. Clay Harris, who lives seven miles northwest of Weston, Missouri. This is his story:

In midsummer of 1903 Mr. Harris, who was then a young man, went one Sunday to the home of D. F. Risk to pay an afternoon call. (Mr. Risk later became his father-in-law.) Mr. Harris was surprised and delighted to find that Cole Younger was there; he and Mr. Risk were old friends. The people sat in the living room talking and listening to Cole's stories. One of the listeners said, "Mr. Younger, did you ever kill a woman?"

Cole moved uneasily and looked at the floor, ill at ease. "Yes," he said finally. "Once when I was riding with Quantrill we passed on horseback through a small town in central Missouri. A number of people came to the windows and doors to stare at us. A window on the second floor of one of the houses was raised and a Negro woman leaned out and glared at us. Then she began to call out vile names. I called to her and said, 'Shut up.' Instead of doing this she continued to use vile language. I warned her again and, when she did not cease, I drew my pistol and fired. She fell out of the window on the ground. We did not stop; we continued to ride. I am now ashamed of what I did that day and rarely ever speak of it. But I have told it today. I won't do it again soon. It is one of the things that a person chooses not to think of."

That closed the conversation. No one asked any questions and he did not add to what he had said.

Now he must get a job. But how?

Finally he got one, selling to farmers a newly invented coal-oil burner. It was a stove fed by coal oil and was supposed to do away with wood and coal. Once more he was behind a horse and buggy, this time in Oklahoma. He would stop at a farmer's house, show a small model of his wonderful stove, and try to talk the farmer into believing that here was one of the great inventions of the ages. The farmers took this great gift to mankind very calmly, more interested in Cole than coal oil. One night he put up at the Rockefellow Hotel on East Broadway, in Muskogee. The word got out that Cole Younger was in town and so many people rushed into the lobby to stare open-mouthed that the manager asked Cole to go upstairs to get rid of the people. No sales. Finally he gave up trying to sell his labor-saving coal-oil stove and returned to Lee's Summit to his comfortable wood fire.

He tried to promote an electric trolley line between Kansas City and Lee's Summit, but once again the people let him give his sales talk just to see him. Finally he gave up this job, too.

Out of a clear sky came an offer from a brewer in Chicago. At this time America was getting a taste of the Wild West Show. Buffalo Bill was making a huge success, and so was Pawnee Bill. The Chicago man said that he would finance an outdoor show to be called the "Cole Younger–Frank James Wild West Show" if he could star Frank James and Cole. Frank was agreeable, but with Cole this was another matter.

His conditional parole said that he should not exhibit himself for money, and Cole meant to stick to it to the letter, for no one was more honest and meticulous in matters of honor than Cole—when he wasn't in hot water. He had lied right and left about the mysterious Howard and Woods, and he had thrown off on Belle Starr, but this was because he wanted to get out of prison. Nothing had been too sacred to interfere with that. And he had got out, by good conduct and by watching his step.

His nephew said, as we talked on the front porch:

"You ask if I know anything about Uncle Cole's Wild West Show. I can answer that by saying I ought to, as I was the treasurer. It was considerably bigger'n most people have the idea, having 120 riders—that's one way to measure an outdoor show. They were made up of cowboys, Indians, and Cossacks. At this time Cossacks were always a feature of a ridin' and shootin' show. In fact, we had more riders than Buffalo Bill. I won't say our show approached his for fame and entertainment, but we had the best riders in the country, and some famous old Indian warriors who were awful hard to cook for, presentin' no end of problems in that line. Frank was to ride and shoot, but Uncle Cole wasn't, as per his pardon agreement. He was 'arena manager.' In carrying out his duties, he would walk through with his big black hat on and if people chose to point him out, that was their privilege. As a matter of fact, people called to him and shouted his name, which salutations he would return, but he didn't do any show tricks, never fired a pistol at Indian or target. However, he had a permit to carry one and this he did, for crooks and panhandlers followed our show like deerflies and they hated Uncle Cole, because he was always on watch. These gentry were not under his control, so he had to do what he could on a personal basis. And this he did by writin' a letter ahead to the chief of police in the next town where we were goin' to exhibit an' tellin' him there was a band of light fingers following the show and battening on it. When the management of the show heard this they were truculent and said he had no right to do this. Uncle Cole said they had no right to short change people an' if the management didn't like it they could jump in the Kaw.

"Had bad luck to start with. Opened in Arkansas and of the first twenty-one days it rained eighteen. Had so much rain that a carnival company, traveling our territory, had to give up the ghost. Some of the time it was difficult for us to pay the riders, but some way or other we managed it somehow.

"I just made mention of the baboons who followed our show. Well, it was my job to collect the money from the ticket wagons and specialty shows. I had a keister and I would put it in that. Dan McCarthy was our chief detective and he went with me, and as we walked along, we would see silent figures lurking in doorways or behind tents. I would take the money to the hotel, keep it there until the next day, then take it to the bank. I never lost a cent from brigandage, but many a night my heart was beatin' like a captured rabbit's. Uncle Cole didn't go with me; he said if he took a shot at a holdup man that it would be spread all over the papers and redound to the discredit of the organization.

"These camp followers became more and more bold. There wasn't any way to contain 'em. They had it in for Frank and Uncle Cole because they wouldn't let these card-sharps draw patrons of the show into crooked card games, a principal source of income to this scum. One day when we were playing a town in northern Texas, Uncle Cole went out for a drive with a local admirer who wanted to show Uncle Cole the town. When Uncle Cole got back, he saw a crowd of toughs milling around Frank, jostling him and workin' themselves up to an open attack. Uncle Cole got out of the landau and walked rapidly toward the rowdies, his hogleg in his hand: 'Hold 'em a minute, Buck,' he called. 'I'll be there and we can re-enact old times.' The ruffians got out of there so fast they didn't even leave tracks. Uncle Cole could have taken care of them, that I am sure of. He was sixty-four then, but he had a good eye and a true finger.

"Uncle Cole joined the Lew Nichols Carnival Company, Frank James not participatin'. Lew Nichols was a good showman an' as straight as a gun barrel, wouldn't allow no sharpers. It was a pleasure to work for him. But he didn't make money, conditions being what they were. Once the show got behind to the extent of $600. Uncle Cole telegraphed the bank here, where he'd built up a deposit, got the money, and pulled the show out of the hole. The money was duly returned to him, for Lew Nichols was a square shooter. 'Colonel' he was mostly called, after the fashion of the day, Missouri being filled with 'colonels' and 'judges.' In fact, Cole's father was called Colonel, but never wore a sword in his life. In fact, once or twice 'Colonel' has been attached to me.

"By the time Uncle Cole had withdrawn from the show, he had saved up enough money to buy a house here in town, not the one where we're sittin', but on Market Street. He gave it to my sister Nora Hall, and there we all lived together. In fact, after he got back from his sojourn in Minnesota I lived in the same house with him until he passed on, a matter of thirteen years."

"Do you," I asked, "remember any anecdote about him?"

He studied for some moments. "One morning we were havin' breakfast. It was raining a sopping drizzle an' everything was wet and damp and soggy. He sat there for some time, just looking out the window at the never-ceasin' rain, not bothering to address me. Then he kind of sighed and said, 'That stuff out there is what put us in the Minnesota pen.' He indicated that him and Jim and Bob and Charlie Pitts would have got away if it hadn't rained so much that they got mired down and couldn't negotiate the swamps.

"When he gave up the Wild West Show he came home and sat around, allowed he was tired. He loved children and they loved him. As soon as he popped his head out the door, they'd come running like he was a Pied Piper, swingin' on his hands and callin' him 'Uncle Cole.' Sometimes he would take one up in his arms and carry her down the street, a meerschaum pipe in his mouth, with now and then a wisp of smoke streaming out behind. Sometimes Frank James would come over, but the children didn't call him Uncle Frank and none of 'em ever swung on his hands.

"There's one incident I must bring out about the Nichols organization. Happened at Richmond, this state, in June 1908. The carnival was a kind of street fair; tents and booths and shooting galleries were set up on the street. Balloon ascensions, too. The carnival was to play from Monday to Saturday. Uncle Cole'd never play on Sunday. Well, when he got there the old-timers flocked around him like kids around a pop'lar teacher. One of them happened to mention that Bloody Bill Anderson had been buried in the potter's field in Richmond. Uncle Cole came to attention. 'Buried in the potter's field!' he said, shocked.

" 'That's right. And he never had a funeral preached over him, either.'

" 'That's a plumb disgrace,' said Uncle Cole. 'That ought to be rectified.'

"He sat there for some minutes, smokin' and thinkin'. 'Why, nobody was ever better friends'n me and Bill. One

time he saved my life, leastways I always gave him credit for
it. Never had a funeral! Why, that ain't Christian. I'll give
him a funeral myself, and I'll preach it, damned if I won't!
We've got two bands and they can play church music. We'll
have a decent funeral tomorrow and I'll preach a sermon
Bloody Bill would be proud to hear.'

"The next morning the two bands came out. James L.
Farris, Junior, was engaged to help, the son of James L.
Farris who was a captain in the Confederate Army and who'd
known Bloody Bill. Bill'd been buried in the Old Cemetery,
no longer used and not too far from the center of town.
Down the street marched the two bands playing softly and
appropriately, half the town walking with them. When they
got to the grave they muffled their drums, and Uncle Cole
stepped forward and said it was a shame that Captain Anderson had had to wait forty-four years to have a funeral
preached over him, but he was goin' to do it. He told what
a good soldier Bill was and how he was acting under orders
from General Sterling Price and couldn't do anything else
than what he was doin'. Then he told how Bill'd been shot
down near the town of Orrick by Yankee scoundrels and that
Bill was a credit, as a soldier and a gentleman, to any county
in the state and that Ray County ought to be mighty proud
to have him interred in its soil. Then he really got going,
Uncle Cole did, and gave all his pent-up hate to war and
the Jayhawkers and Red Legs. The latter was safe; in Richmond I don't reckon there was half-a-dozen Union sympathizers. When Uncle Cole got through, you had a lot
more respect for Bill and for Uncle Cole, too, for that matter.
Then Elder J. E. Dunn, who was a well-known preacher,
stepped forward and offered a prayer over Bill, very touching. Finally it was all over and the people started down the

street, the band played softly. I don't reckon, in the state of Missouri, there was ever preached a finer, more sincere funeral sermon than Uncle Cole preached over Bloody Bill."

I wanted to see if there was any documentary evidence to support what Mr. Hall had told me, and I found there was and that what he had told me was substantially correct. I found two "write-ups" of the show and one of the funeral in the *Richmond Missourian*, June 4 and June 11, 1908. First there was an offer from the carnival management of One Thousand Dollars (their capitals) to anyone who could prove that the Cole Younger with the company was not the original Cole Younger, "last of the famous Younger brothers." Also I found some fascinating facts about the kind of show a carnival company put on in those days. Here is a list of its "attractions":

The Old Plantation
The Live Octopus
The Den of Horrors
Mysterious Edna
The Girl from Dixie
Trapeze by Beatty and Irene Miller
Cole Younger's Coliseum
Balloon Ascension by "Aeronautress" Lucy May Colton.
    "She jumps from the clouds and comes down head first in a way that thrills and chills."
The 85-foot-high dive from the top of a ladder into a net by the Great Colton. "It is a thoroughly sensational act. Bring the children."

Which gives an idea what entertainment was like in Missouri in 1908.

PERSONAL. It was shortly after this that the Cole Younger

Carnival came to my home town in Missouri. They set up in Prather's Pasture at the edge of town. I was among the gapers when Cole walked by. He was a large man with, it seemed to me, an unusually large face. Little did I dream that someday I would be writing a book about him.

One of our neighbors had brought in a wagonload of watermelons. He had taken his team off the wagon and hitched it nearby. He had two barrels of ice water and in these barrels he cooled off the melons. Night came, and darkness took over, except for the acetylene torches. Some of the gentry connected with the carnival untied the farmer's horses, gave them a larrup, and yelled "Whoa! Whoa!" Our neighbor ran after them, also yelling "Whoa! Whoa!" The carnival company descended on the melons, stealing them right and left. After a time the farmer came back, the maddest man in the Platte Purchase.

Finally Cole Younger and his carnival left. A lot of our people muttered that they'd better never come back.

I'll set down here an anecdote or two that illustrate phases of Cole Younger's complex character. The first is from L. Mitchell White, editor of the *Mexico Ledger*, Mexico, Missouri. He wrote me:

You'll be interested to know that Cole Younger once was on the other side of the law—August 1, 1912. This was a big day in Lee's Summit, Missouri—William Jennings Bryan, the Boy Orator of the Platte, lectured to a Chautauqua audience. The audience was swept off its feet by his fire and oratory. When the lecture was over, Cole found that his wallet, containing $95, had been stolen. Cole was swept off his feet, too, and uttered oratory to the effect that he'd just like to get his hands on the low-down thief. I've often wondered what would have happened if Cole had found him. Sets the imagination winging, doesn't it?

From Roy D. Williams, Boonville, Missouri:

When the Wild West show was running, Cole and Frank came to our town. Our livery stable sent its best team down to the railroad depot to meet the two notables. On the way back, the carriage containing the two men came to the corner where our bank was located. Cole said, "Frank, we ought to get our big bills changed into small money. Come on, we'll go in and do that."

Frank thought for a moment, then said, "If Cole Younger and Frank James walk into that bank together, they'll slam the vault door and begin shooting."

The matter was settled by Cole and Frank holding the lines while the driver went in to get the bills changed.

Cole began to feel that carnival life was too much for him; he'd outlasted Frank James in it; and now Cole gave it up. He said he wanted to loaf. This was his life for a while. He would come downtown in the middle of the morning and go into the hotel lobby where he had a special chair. If a stranger popped into it, why, the regulars popped him out! On pleasant days they would carry a chair out on the sidewalk and there Cole would sit, his big black hat tipped back on his head, smoking his long-stemmed German pipe. Now and then a child would come and climb up into his lap. Cole liked to talk politics. He was an ardent Democrat. About this time the papers came out with the news that Frank James was going to vote the Republican ticket. When he heard the extraordinary news, Cole was stunned. "I think Buck must be out of his mind," he said. Cole liked to talk about what he called "my brush days," but would say nothing at all about his outlaw days.

One of his great pleasures was to attend a Quantrill picnic when the men who had ridden with Quantrill would meet, place a great framed picture of Quantrill on a special stand,

and talk about "the old days." Cole would never admit that
Quantrill had lied to them and misled them and that he was
the worst butcher America had ever known. To Cole he was
still "Captain Quantrill," and he spoke the name with respect. Sometimes, at these rallies, Cole would speak; when he
sat down there was always a great clapping of hands, for his
old comrades liked him and completely forgave him for his
forays against the banks and railroads. When the meeting
was over Cole would lead them in the Rebel yell and then,
one by one, the old guerrillas would hobble out to the picnic
tables.

Cole wanted to "make up" for what he had done . . . if he
could only make people see that a life of crime, which looked
so exciting, was, in reality, a life of tragedy. And so he went
out on a lecture tour. Rowland Marquette, 618 South Miller
Street, Lee's Summit, told me about it:

"I was his manager. My wife was his grand-niece, so I was
sort of a member of the family. I took Uncle Cole out on
two trips altogether, and we traveled through six states—
Oklahoma, Arizona, New Mexico, Arkansas, some of Kentucky, and part of Texas. The lecture lasted about an hour
and a quarter. He would tell his experiences in the war and
his days in prison. He was leading up to what he called the
'moral' of his talk and this was that crime does not pay. When
he reached this part of his lecture his voice trembled and he
put a fervor into his talk that took hold of people. If he saw
a boy in the audience, he would direct his talk at him. If the
boy came up after the lecture to ask questions, he would drop
everybody else and direct all his attention to him. Sometimes, when we were on the train, he would rouse himself
out of deep thought and say with a plaintive note, 'If I could
only make the boys understand.' "

The lectures began to tell on Cole and he complained

about feeling heavy and logy. "I guess my lead is pulling me down," he would say. He had reason to speak of this for fourteen bullets still reposed in him.

More and more he talked of the past and he spoke of old friends. But most of them were gone. He was lonely, and when someone stopped him on the street, he was delighted; or when he was invited to a home and he could sit, after supper and smoke his pipe, that was nice, too.

A revivalist came to Lee's Summit. Cole was asked to attend the meetings, but he had said he didn't take any "stock" in preachers. Finally, to please his niece, he went. At first he was restless, then centered his attention on what the minister was saying. The next night Cole went back; and the next and the next. Finally, the word went out that Cole "had seen the light." One night, when converts were called for, Cole got up and walked slowly forward, his large frame almost filling the aisle of the little church. He stood a moment at the chancel rail, then said in a firm voice, "I want to repent my sins and join the church."

The people were so touched, so moved by the change that had come over the old outlaw, that they stood up as a body and applauded—an almost unheard-of matter in the Christian church.

After the service was over, the people flocked around him, shaking his hand. When he spoke there was a quaver in his voice. "I don't know why I didn't do this long ago. I was with God in my youth, then I deserted Him. Now I am back."

And he meant it. He was baptized and attended services regularly. He spoke to the boys who came to see him and advised them to go to church. But the boys wanted him to show them how he handled a pistol. This he would not do.

He continued faithfully to go to church. Sometimes, as

the preacher talked, Cole put his hand behind his ear and leaned forward; sometimes, after the regular sermon, he spoke and each time put into it the lesson he believed so deeply—that crime does not pay.

Instead of going to the hotel lobby, which was a sort of headquarters for him, he began more and more to stay at home. He had a room on the second floor and there he would sit in a rocking chair, smoking his long pipe and looking out the window. When a child passed, Cole would wave delightedly.

One day exceedingly bad news came. After giving up the carnival, Frank James had gone to Fletcher, Oklahoma, to farm, but it hadn't worked out well, and so he returned to the old home place where he had been born, about forty miles from where Cole was living. Now and then the two old warriors got together; their voices would rumble along, then suddenly laughter would ring out. When anyone came up they changed the subject. But now came word that Frank was "poorly." But Cole was "poorly," too, and could not go to see him. Finally word came, February 18, 1915, that Frank had "passed on." According to his nephew, Cole hardly mentioned Frank's death all day. "He just went upstairs by himself and sat there."

Word got out that Cole was ill and his old guerrilla friends came to see him, getting out of cars now. The doctor would not let them see him, but the fact that they had come to see him cheered Cole up. When they were not admitted, the old guerrillas would go to the hotel lobby and sit around and "visit." Now and then Cole's name would be mentioned; there would be a little pause in the conversation, then they would begin to talk again.

Cole revived and seemed stronger. He sent for Harry C. Hoffman and Jesse James, Junior—said he wanted to "talk."

The two men drove by car from Kansas City together and went up the stairs. Cole was propped up in bed, smoking his long-stemmed pipe. He seemed to be anxious to talk and told what had happened at Northfield, the first time he had ever told it, he said, and asked them not to reveal what he had confided. Jesse, Junior, died without telling. Mr. Hoffman lives in Oxford, Ohio. He has never revealed what was told that day as Cole smoked and talked.

The house became a kind of shrine for the old guerrillas; they could no longer see Cole but they would ride past, looking up at his window, hoping to catch a glimpse of their old captain.

The doctor made him give up his pipe. "I understand," said Cole.

He knew the end was coming, but he met it as he had faced death so many times. He was steadily growing weaker from uremia and a complication of diseases, including heart trouble. He called his nieces and nephews into the room; they gathered around his bed, but he was too weak to tell them something that evidently had been on his mind. He died at a quarter of nine at night, February 21, 1916, aged seventy-two, the last of the great outlaws.

The Quantrill men tried to muster up enough old friends to act as honorary pallbearers, but they were too feeble. Two of the grizzled old veterans sat in cars outside the church; now and then they called him "Captain." The honorary pallbearers finally selected were his friends, all younger men, not the ones who had ridden with him so many years ago, in an age that seemed incredibly far away. One of the pallbearers was Jesse James, Junior; another was Frank James's son, Robert F. James. Present also was Mrs. Frank James, now a widow.

Todd M. George told me that he went to the church two

hours before the time set for the funeral; the church was already filled, with people standing in the yard, talking in hushed voices.

Cole was buried in the family plot, beside his mother, with Jim and Bob. Not one now of the Younger boys was living.

The grave has two stones, which is a bit unusual in itself. The one set up by the family reads:

COLE YOUNGER

1844   1916

Rest in Peace

Our Dear Beloved

A second stone, placed beside the first by the Confederate States of America, reads:

CAPTAIN COLE YOUNGER

CAPT. QUANTRILL'S CO.

C. S. A.

CHAPTER XVI

The Author Visits Belle Starr's Grave.
The End of Pearl Younger

I was eager to see Belle Starr's grave with my own eyes, for no one I'd ever met had seen it, so inaccessible, so remote is it. In fact, there hadn't been a description of it printed in twenty years.

I went to Eufaula, Oklahoma, and there asked how I could get to the grave. No one knew and not one soul did I find who'd ever been there. One man, Robert Simpson, told me, "As a boy I used to see Belle Starr come here on horseback for groceries. She had a splint basket on her arm, and two pistols in her belt."

"Dean Parkhurst can get you there if anybody can," I was told.

I hunted up Dean Parkhurst, the town's photographer.

"I don't know where the grave is, but we can try," he said cheerfully.

Arrangements were made to set off into the hills. We entered his car, me quite excited; the car coughed and moved slowly out of the driveway. At the edge of town it coughed ominously and lay down in the middle of the road; at least it seemed that way to me, for it would not move. Finally, with the help of kindhearted people, we got it back to Eufaula. Dean raced around and finally came back with a pickup truck, the noisiest piece of mechanism for its size on the face of the earth, and we set forth once more. In no time at all we were lost.

We met an Indian trudging along the road and asked him where Belle Starr's grave was.

The old Indian, with the wisdom of the ages in his face, said, "Don't know," and trudged on.

The country became more desolate and forlorn. Now and then we would see, tucked in the timber, a dilapidated cabin. "Sharecroppers. Cotton mostly," said Dean. "We haven't had crops for four years. That's the reason the Government is going to put in a dam on the South Canadian River and irrigate this whole section. This is a fine section, if we can get water. Used to be very prosperous."

Finally, by asking here and there, we arrived at Porum, a town that will not have traffic problems for years to come. We stopped a man on the street and asked how we could get to Belle's grave.

"You'll have to see the barber first," he said, and went his way.

Shortly we found ourselves at the barbershop of Claude A. Hamilton. He was in his shirt sleeves, had on a green eyeshade, and was working away at a customer's hair.

We introduced ourselves.

"I bought the grave an' forty acres of land at a delinquent tax sale. But I don't allow tourists."

Hurt by the implications, I explained that we were not tourists.

"You are to me," said Mr. Hamilton firmly.

"In fact," I said, still suffering from the wound, "Mr. Parkhurst is one of the Eufaula officials for the new power site on the Canadian River."

That helped, definitely.

"He is working with the United States Government," I added, seeing the wind had changed.

"Why do you want to go there?" Mr. Hamilton asked, only half in our net.

"I've heard so much about the grave that I want to see it with my own eyes. I want to write something about it."

"Then you'll make money on it?"

"A little," I said with the conviction of a man who knows what he is talking about.

"I have no use for tourists," he said with ill-concealed disgust. "One time I was there—mind you, on my own property —and a tourist took a hammer out of his pocket and began to chip off part of the upright slab. I ordered him to stop. He threatened to throw me off my property. Then I told him to get off and I walked toward him and he knew I meant it. That's the kind of people we get wantin' to see Belle's grave."

"I understand," I murmured.

"I don't allow anybody to go to the grave. In two or three years I'm goin' to put in a road and signs to the grave and open it to the public. The new power site will bring in a lot of people and I'll cash in on the property. The water, when the dam is finished, will cover all that section but won't cover Belle's grave, it bein' on a sort of raised knoll, or hummock you might call it. Maybe people can row out to see her grave. But they'd have to pay just like anybody else. That's what I've got in mind. Next."

The customer moved out and a man sitting in an upright chair against the wall got up and took his place.

"As per usual?"

"Yes."

I urged Mr. Hamilton again.

"Well, all right, but you'll have to take a guide. I want

everybody under supervision. I'll also send my daughter Lois. Mind you, both will have to be paid."

We all piled into the noisy pickup truck and set out on the crookedest trail I'd seen in years. The country grew wilder and wilder.

"What do people do for a living through here?" I asked.

"Farm, mostly, unless they're on relief."

"That's the Cole Younger School," said Lois. "Our teacher lets us take our shoes off."

"It's properly the Younger's Bend School," said the guide, "but most people call it the Cole Younger School."

We came to a trail that led off through the wilderness. "This is where we get out. We'll have to hoof it the rest of the way," the guide said cheerfully. "That's the Belle Starr Canyon, that's the Belle Starr Spring, and there's the cave where they hid their horses. The old-timers say when she took over from Big Head, there was only one cabin, then she built two more, all connectin' and strung out. There used to be a story she had a piano, but it was only talk. No way to get a piano in. Her and her friends used to hole up here and have high old times. The officers knew where they were but were not eager to challenge them. All the Starrs through here backed her up and they're as thick as lightning bugs on a June night. There ain't any authentic record she ever killed anybody, but she might have, people in them days not prone to talk more'n necessary. I guess no other place in the United States ever had as many rough characters under one roof as Belle's had. Queer woman, but lots of people liked her, had a big heart, devoted to her daughter Pearl. Had a son Ed, but never doted on him like she did on Pearl. Here's where the cabins stood, kind of anti-godlin' off in this direction. All gone now. And here's the remains of her grave, as you can see."

There it was, a mound of earth housed around with slabs of stone, the whole thing surrounded by barbed wire and pole fence.

"Watch out for poison ivy," said the guide. "The place is badly neglected. Belle could play a piano and was an accomplished horse thief. She was a Missouri lady and, in her early days, was a spy for the South. The stone, with her epitaph, used to stand up here at her head. Was in white and elegantly carved. But the slab has disappeared."

"It's under Daddy's bed," said little Lois.

After we had stayed awhile—me thinking of the stories the grave could tell—we all slogged back to the pickup truck, entered it, and rumbled down the mountain trail.

We met an Indian on a pony. The Indian pulled the pony to the side of the road.

"Hello, Joe," called the guide. The Indian nodded. "Farms back in the woods. Don't hardly ever come to town. Never has been on relief."

"This is my daddy's house," said Lois proudly.

I peered out at a mountaineer cabin set in the brush.

"Can we see the headstone?" I asked.

"We'll have to ask Mama."

A woman came to the door. "You'll have to pull it out yourself. It's heavy, what's left of it."

The guide got the two pieces out—all that is left of the stone that stood over Belle's grave—and carried them into the yard.

"Claude always says the tourists chipped it to pieces," said the guide. "But didn't many tourists get there. I think the cattle knocked it over and broke it. But somebody did carry away some of the pieces. These two are all that's left. Claude is goin' to set them in place again when he opens it up, after the dam is in, for tourists."

We took photographs and got ready to leave. Lois got into the truck with us.

"Tell your daddy to come home early. I have something special tonight," called the girl's mother as she stood in the door of the mountain cabin.

We rattled past the Cole Younger School, finally got back to Porum, and went to the barbershop. Mr. Hamilton in his green eyeshade was still working away.

"It's a great sight, ain't it? Everybody tells me I'll make a handsome thing of it, when the dam is in. Now you can pay your guides, like I mentioned."

I gave Lois a dollar. Her eyes shone. "I'm goin' to show it to my teacher," she said.

After a time I was back in the pickup and soon the pickup was bounding down the road. Many things were in my mind, and many were in Dean Parkhurst's, too, for he said, "You don't see things like that every day. You just wouldn't hardly think it was America today, would you?"

Belle Starr had a deep and moving love for Pearl Younger. Her greatest desire was for Pearl to be a "lady"—to live a vastly different life from the one she herself had led. Once, for a time, she had hoped that Pearl would be a great actress; when this fell to pieces she hoped that Pearl would marry a rich man and live a life of ease and luxury.

When Belle was in prison, Pearl lived with her grandmother and grandfather Reed who did not want her to be known as Younger and changed her name to Reed in honor of their own name, her stepfather's, and her half-brother's. Their family nickname for her was "Rosie" or "Rosa," and thus, for the time, she was Rosa Reed.

After Belle's return to Younger's Bend, Pearl was again Pearl Younger and as long as Belle lived Pearl was Pearl

Younger. After her mother's death, Pearl changed it to Pearl Starr, but Belle Starr's name became in the popular mind such a black one that Pearl went back to her childhood name of Reed.

There was a streak of wildness in this child of such bizarre parents and she went to Fort Smith and into what was known as "The Row." Finally she moved out of this and established a "house" of her own on North First Street. It had over the entryway a glass fan, or lunette, and in this was a star—a strange tribute from a daughter to her mother. Also, when her mother died, Pearl had had carved on the tombstone a star and a bell.

She married a man named William Harrison, but soon was divorced. It was not long until she had a child—father unknown—whom she called "Flossie." The child was promptly put among relatives and her parentage hidden. It was not until many years later that Flossie found out that Pearl was her mother and Belle Starr her grandmother. Flossie wrote some lurid Sunday newspaper pieces about her grandmother, using, for the most part, material from the *National Police Gazette*. And then she disappeared; I do not know what became of her.

Pearl went from one admirer to another—this woman who had once been the Canadian Lily—and finally moved West where she died in Douglas, Arizona, July 8, 1925, and is buried in Calvary Cemetery in that city under the name of Rosa Reed. The death certificate says, "daug of Belle Starr."

CHAPTER XVII

Myths and Legends

COLE had the unique experience of becoming a legend while he was living. After he left Minnesota—the man who came to help himself to a feast and stayed twenty-five years— he returned to Missouri, as we've seen. But he was no more than there before a man popped up in the state of Washington who said he was the real Cole Younger. Not only this, but the man went on the lecture platform and told of his outlaw days in Missouri. Cole, properly incensed, said he would like to meet that man just once; the implication was that Cole would end the man's public career then and there. The man got so much newspaper space that when Cole went out with his Wild West Show the management advertised it would pay $1,000 to anyone who could prove that their Cole wasn't the real article. People would crowd up to Cole, when he was with the show, and say, "Are you really Cole Younger?"

Cole, always a little peeved by this, would answer sharply, "Of course I am," and turn and walk away.

A tale that has been told a thousand times is that Cole joined Quantrill because Cole's father had been killed and robbed by Jayhawkers, and Cole wanted revenge. Cole himself told it—a little acting here. The truth is that Cole joined Quantrill nine months before the father was killed. But Cole's account made a good story; no one, with any milk of human kindness in his veins, could hear it without getting all stirred up.

One of the favorite inventions was "the Southern soldier" story. Once, so the story went, when the passengers on a train were contributing to the grain sack, one of the men said, "I am a poor man and this is all the money I have. I served two years under General Sterling Price."

"Which company?" asked Cole.

The man told him.

"I can't take money from anybody who served under General Sterling Price," said Cole. "Keep your money and add this to it." He dipped into the grain sack, and fished out a bill and handed it to the man.

This story was told around countless stoves in my part of Missouri. The unfortunate thing is there is no evidence that Cole ever gave back a penny to anybody, either ex-soldier or ordinary man.

A story with different ruffles on it was told about a stage robbery in Texas. The passengers were lined up outside the stagecoach and Cole and his comrades were dangling the grain sack enticingly in front of them when one of the men said, "I'm a preacher and I am a poor man."

"Oh!" said Cole. "We certainly don't want to rob a preacher. Stand over there."

The man stepped out of the group and thus escaped the unpleasantries.

Another story was that Cole, as he relieved passengers of their surplus money, would quote Bible verses. This was not true. During his "riding" days Cole was not of a religious nature, but later, as we've seen, he became a sincerely devout man and obtained a peace of mind that he'd never known before.

A story was spread that he was a pious fraud and as tricky as a gypsy horse trader, but this wasn't true. No one was more honest and less pretentious than Cole—that is, in the latter part of his life. When he was still in the saddle he lied right and left in order to have suspicion turned from him; and this was true when he was imprisoned in Minnesota. He wanted to get out, and he pretended to be more than he was. But he wasn't pious and he wasn't pretentious.

Another story that went around was that he had buried a vast sum of money. Also not true. In fact, he made very little money as a robber. When he was brought down in Minnesota he had about $50 and that was all the money he had in the world. He had started to Minnesota with $300; he had won and lost some of it gambling; out of what remained he had bought his horse. This was the general financial situation with the other men, too, for they were expecting to fill their pockets in Minnesota. No pockets were filled, but some hides were.

Much was made of the fact that the Youngers were related to the Dalton boys; there was bad blood in the family, people said. The relationship was remote; Cole was a second cousin to the Dalton boys. There is no evidence that he ever saw them. The Dalton boys were younger, and did not come into prominence until Cole was paling in prison.

A hard-to-down legend was that the Youngers were related to the Jameses, but this is not true.

Strangely enough, there have never been tall tales about Cole's marksmanship; many about Jesse's. And yet, so far as I know, Cole was as neat with a pistol as Jesse.

One of the favorite stories about Cole was that when he captured a Union sympathizer—if he let him live—he made him take the Black Oath. The trouble with this is that there was no Black Oath, and there was no Black Flag. In fact, a motion picture was made dealing with the life of Cole Younger; it was called *Under the Black Flag*. And so runs the world of legend.

CHAPTER XVIII

Summary. What Kind of Man Was He?

As a boy I lived not far from the Bandit Belt and grew up on stories of the James-Youngers. We had a well in our yard and in the well was an iron pump. It was my duty, the last thing at night, to go out and pump a bucket of fresh water. I would dash out and work the handle like mad, for I could see Jesse James behind the clothes pole, and I could see Cole Younger holding the horses in the drive lot. The fact that Jesse was in his grave and Cole in the pen didn't lessen the danger. They were bad men who wanted to slit my throat so quietly Pa couldn't hear a squeak. Then, with the bucket filled, I would dash back into the house with the speed of Jesse James on horseback.

They were bad men, and that was all there was to it, I thought. But as I grew older and learned more about them, I began to realize that in their lives and careers there were ameliorating conditions and I began to see how their times affected them. They were sons of circumstance.

One of the stories about Cole was that he, as a boy, loved to torture animals. I believed it and many people believed it. I didn't know then that this was the standard opening of most of the lurid books of the day. It was not until much later I found that he was, in reality, a rather admirable boy. He was a school leader and was what in those days was called a "good scholar." He was normal in every way; he hunted and fished and was mighty with a musket, as were all the boys in this section. When the conflict between Missouri and Kansas broke out—the dreadful Border War—Cole was still a boy, but he became involved. The Younger family were Southerners, but Cole's father did not believe in slavery—a shaky position. Meantime the Border War was coming closer and closer and Cole was drawn into it. He got into it early. When he was nineteen he was riding with Quantrill. When he was bent upon killing, he gave the Rebel yell and became half-insane with the fever of killing. He did not kill except when on a raid, or when avenging the murder of his father. But even during this time a bit of ethics was still in him. He was not greatly different from a thousand other farm boys in this section.

When the War Between the States was over and he returned to his county, he rode into a new situation. The Confederates had had many rights taken from them. Villages had been destroyed, farmhouses burned, fields which had once raised corn were now weed patches. The spirit of war and carnage lay over the land like a swamp fog. At night bands of ex-soldiers fired into the homes of Southern sympathizers. Everybody was more or less a brigand—these very men who had once been comradely farm boys.

Cole had no money to buy horses with which to farm. He was at a loss what to do. Certain jobs were denied men who had fought for the South; such a man could not teach school; he could not preach a sermon; he could not run for public office. The boys who had ridden together now met in secret groups; the world they had known was no more. They needed money; they were used to violence and carnage. They decided to rob a bank—everybody hated banks. It probably did not seem worse to Cole to rob a bank than it was to rob a Federal storehouse. He was twenty-two.

The robbery was miraculously easy. He rode off to Texas in high spirits. It was not long until he again needed money. This, too, was a success. And now he could not turn back. His natural ability made him a leader. The band became famous and Cole Younger became, at an early age, a famous outlaw.

However, some bit of conscience still clung to him, like a raveling on a sleeve. He tried to give up this kind of life. But not quite earnestly enough.

Now comes a puzzler: if he had come from the war onto a farm and into a living, would he have turned bandit? Or was there already some breach in his moral wall that would have made him an outlaw, come what might? Are we all children of circumstances? Or have we each some protective envelope that allows, like a blood cell, no false entry? I have puzzled over this long, but I have no ready answer.

Now and then he was accused of taking part in a robbery when he had not been there. He still wanted to have a good name—that much of the ravel was still there—and protested violently that he was innocent. He went to great lengths to get the names of people who could swear that he had not been present at the robbery; nobody ever threw more dust than Cole did. But, as noted, when he was guilty he kept as quiet as a quail in a covert. Never a cheep.

He became more and more involved in horse and holster work. He kept planning on what he would do when he got out. One of his dreams was to go to South America and become a ranchman.

And then came the fiasco at Northfield. The moment he was clapped into prison he began planning how to get out; indeed he began planning it before the doors even closed on him. He hid facts, he lied unconscionably, he toadied and pussyfooted; he was going to get himself out somehow. And he did, with the help of the amazing Bronaugh.

The moment he was out, he settled back into the man he had been in his early days. He was honest, his word was reliable. After he got out of prison he never turned a questionable dollar. In fact, he wanted robbers sent to prison as fast as wheels would take them.

He had a dual nature: he was frank and he was secretive. He had many friends and he seemed to take them to his heart. But at the same time there was a wall over which they were never allowed to peep.

As he grew older he became more and more pontifical. He bulked large and he talked slowly and, often, dully. He liked to utter platitudes. Was it possible that this puffy man with a large nose and bags under his eyes and with a slow, ponderous way of moving was the mad dog who had killed at Lawrence and who had shot bank cashiers with never a blink?

He had, however, many straight arrows in his quiver. He revered his father, he loved his mother, and he was protective to his brothers. His affection for, and his loyalty to, Frank James were touching. He had, as I have pointed out, none of these for Jesse. He could have shot Jesse and slept well that night.

Religion came into his later life and he got solace from it. He rarely spoke of his outlaw days, and when he did he told no detail, gave no information. When he became a lecturer he delicately entitled his lecture "What Life Has Taught Me"—not, as one would think, "My Life in Crime." In his lectures he was exceedingly earnest in his denunciation of crime. And he meant it.

One thing puzzles me and this was his attitude toward the indomitable Bronaugh, after Cole got out of prison. Cole lived not too far from his rescuer, but he never went to see him and he rarely mentioned him. Why Cole should take this aloof and impersonal attitude I do not know.

Why should he survive in public interest when others of his time faded away and were no more? One reason is that he was such a dominant figure that the band became the James-Younger outlaws. Another is that he lived longer than any of them; he became a showman, a lecturer, and continued to be in the public eye long after the other pistol men were forgotten.

A question arises: why isn't Cole as famous as Jesse? (He killed more men than Jesse did.) One reason is that Cole lacked a tongue-tickling name; another is that Jesse died dramatically at the hands of a traitor, and Cole was unlucky enough to die in bed.

If the war had not come upon him, Cole would probably have gone into politics. He was always interested in them; he was a fairly good speaker and could, when occasion was right, extend a glad hand. In fact, while he was in prison he said in a newspaper interview that people should study their Bible and the president's messages. Cole was being a bit sanctimonious here, for there is no evidence that he, at this time, ever opened the Bible. But he did read the presidential messages—very dull reading, I have no doubt.

Sometimes I have the sinking feeling that Cole was just the average man caught in a melon patch.

Sources

The dates in this chapter have been taken, for the most part, from a small book written by Cole Younger entitled *The Story of Cole Younger. By Himself,* published in 1903 in Chicago by the Henneberry Company. The book is devoted chiefly to the matter of telling what a misunderstood man he was. He tells quite honestly about his days as a warrior, but when he moves over to banks and railroads he is completely unreliable. When he was innocent, he shouted to high heaven; when he was guilty, he covered up.

Cole himself gives the names of his teachers. Both were important in his life. Also Warren C. Bronaugh, in his book *The Youngers' Fight for Freedom,* tells about Cole's teachers.

In his book, Cole tells the story of the ill-fated dance at Cuthbert Mockbee's. The house is still standing and is a famous local landmark; it is brick and well preserved. It is now owned and occupied by Mrs. Martha Stuart Johnson. Henry W. Younger is buried about a mile from the Mockbee house in East Cemetery.

For information about Quantrill, the author has relied on William Elsey Connelley's detailed book *Quantrill and the Border Wars* and on Jay Monaghan's *Civil War on the Western Border.*

Six Mile Church got its name from the fact that it was six miles east of Independence.

Some of the information about Cole's early days came from his nephew Harry Younger Hall, who was named after Cole. I talked to him on his front porch at 506 East Third Street, Lee's Summit; as we swayed gently back and forth in his swing, he told me about "Uncle Cole." It made Cole Younger come alive to me. Mr. Hall lived in the same house with Cole for thirteen years. Mr. Hall, when I visited with him, was eighty-three. He will appear later in our story. Frank Fristoe Talley, who lives in Lee's Summit, told me: "Cole's mother and my grandmother were sisters. My middle name came from the Fristoe side of the family. My great-grandfather, Richard Martin Fristoe, was the first judge of Jackson County. The year was 1827. So the Fristoes have been in this county a long time."

Roy Dunning, Lee's Summit, told me this story which was passed along to him by his grandfather, James C. Worthington: One day, when Cole was a boy, he was building a fence when a band of Jennison's Red Legs rode up. One of them said, "That's too good a team for a boy your age. We'll take them." The men stripped the harness off and rode away leading the horses.

As to family relationships: Adelaide Younger was a daughter of Charles F. Younger. She married the Dalton boys' father, which made Cole and the Dalton boys second cousins. The Daltons were younger than Cole; there is no record that Cole ever met them.

<h2 style="text-align:center">CHAPTER 2</h2>

The details of the murder of Henry Younger and the amount of money involved are from Cole Younger's book. The body was taken in charge by Captain Everett Peabody, who was in command of the militia. He was the one who found the money. Captain Walley was arrested but brought in friends who proved he was some place else, and he was freed.

Cole says, in his brief autobiography, that he was a private in the state guard under General Price. Quantrill was in Captain Stewart's company of cavalry and was then practically unknown.

The information about Cole saving Major Emory S. Foster's life is from Cole's book and from a letter that Major Foster wrote Warren C. Bronaugh, which appears in Bronaugh's book, page 35.

Major Foster was in command of 750 and for one whole day fought a Confederate force of 3,000. If he hadn't been wounded he would have won the battle. He never completely recovered from his wound. His company was Company C, 27th Missouri Infantry. This information comes from a study of him published in the *Missouri Historical Review*, Vol. 14, Numbers 3-4, beginning on page 425. (This is not the last of him that we will have in this book, for suddenly and dramatically he again came into Cole's life.) He died in Oakland, California, in 1902 and was buried in a military plot owned by the G. A. R. where his grave may be seen today.

The story of Steve Elkins appears in Cole's autobiography, also in John McCorkle's book, and was related by Elkins himself when heaven and earth were being moved to get Cole out of the Minnesota prison.

The details of how Cole's mother had to set her own house on fire were related by Cole to Harry C. Hoffman, who passed them along to me.

After the Civil War, the Jayhawk was taken up and became an emblem of the state of Kansas. The cartoon of the bird was originated by Henry Maloy, who was a junior at the University of Kansas. He proudly proclaimed it as "the only bird that wore shoes."

NOTE OF WARNING: A book dealing with the Youngers is *The Life, Character and Daring Exploits of the Younger Brothers*, by August C. Appler, copyrighted first in 1875 and published in later editions. On the title page he says he was editor, for a time, of the *Osceola Democrat*. He invented, wholly and completely, incidents about the Youngers. He picked up and passed along the Richard K. Fox story about Cole killing fifteen prisoners. From the same source he got the story about Cole killing his cousin, "Captain Charles Younger"; Cole had no cousin by the name of Younger in Missouri. He passed along the Fox invention about Cole walking barefooted for half a mile in the winter on a plank fence to escape Union soldiers; this was so they couldn't see his footprints in the snow—an impossible situation. So I beg all who want to know the facts about the Youngers not to rely upon Appler. Appler did have some correspondence with William Dickerson, a man in Floyd, Louisiana, who sheltered Cole for three months.

The story of the apple woman was also related to me by Cole's nephew as we swayed in the porch swing. "It was one of Uncle Cole's favorite stories. He used to chuckle as he told it."

CHAPTER 3

The origin of the story about the silken cord is from John N. Edwards who was so vastly prejudiced that he can't be wholly believed. We shall see later what he said about Cole Younger. Once he made Cole out as innocent as a dewy-eyed bride.

I sent the episode about the scalps to Elmer L. Pigg, Orrick, Missouri, who is the authority on Bloody Bill and his wild ways. Elmer writes: "I don't accept the scalps story. The guerrillas never killed women; it was a kind of code. The men in this day wore their hair to their shoulders, and it is possible that Bloody Bill's father had such scalps on his bridle and people mistook them for women's."

The part about Quantrill being a horse thief is chiefly from Jay Monaghan's book *Civil War on the Western Border*.

The story about Bloody Bill's father is from *Border Ruffian Trouble in Kansas*, by Charles R. Green, page 52.

The details of the killing of the guerrilla girls were sent to me in a letter by George Caleb Bingham's granddaughter, Mrs. Clara K. Bowdry, 1323 Clover Lane, Fort Worth 7, Texas. She, in turn, got them from a letter that her grandfather wrote to the *Washington Sentinel*, date of publication not established. In this letter is much detail, given by Bingham himself, as to how the building was constructed and how girders and pillars were used. He blamed his ancient enemy, General Ewing, for weakening the building with holes in the joists and the removal of wooden pegs. But Bingham was so bitter toward General Ewing that whatever he says about Ewing has to be held up to the light.

It should be pointed out that after Jim Lane escaped he came back and, rallying some men around him, helped chase Quantrill out of the county. Also it should be mentioned that Jim Lane nominated Abraham Lincoln for president in the latter's second campaign.

The story of the mayor is by an eyewitness of the sacking of Lawrence: the Reverend Richard Cordley, who was pastor of the Plymouth Congregational Church in Lawrence. He wrote a book entitled *A History of Lawrence, Kansas, from the First Settlement to the Close of the Rebellion,* published in 1895, in Lawrence, and now a collector's item. In this book appears the story of the mayor.

<h2 style="text-align:center">CHAPTER 4</h2>

Cole tells briefly in his book of sending the money to Bastrop, Louisiana.

His brush with the Comanches is mentioned by himself.

The parts about the parishes he went to in Texas are from his own book, pages 57 and 67. This book has been reliable as to dates and events. But now a new phase of his life begins and Cole forgets to make a memorandum of many things.

In his book Cole got a little mixed up and called General Benjamin McCulloch, General Henry G. McCulloch. This is understandable, for he was writing thirty years after the event, and a lot of blood had flowed under the bridge.

The date of the Liberty bank robbery is usually given as Saint Valentine's Day, February 14. This is wrong. The robbery was the day before, February 13. This is attested by the written statement made shortly afterward by Greenup Bird, the cashier. The handwritten statement still exists and can be seen by those who wish. He, too, is the authority for the amount of money taken. Some of the money was in Government bonds. Frank James's mother had borrowed money from the bank; when time came for repayment she showed up at the bank with revenue stamps which had been stolen that day from the bank. They were not accepted. Mrs. James, who was something of a "character," was highly indignant with the bank.

The James farm was twelve miles from the bank. The building stands today, but is used as an insurance office, with the northwest corner used as a gift shop. I went into the vault where the money was kept, and succeeded in knocking down a whole row of ladies' dresses.

I did not get to Dallas, Texas, so I wrote to the Dallas Public Library to find out about Scyene; back came a letter from Miss Allie Marie Stanley. Says she: "Scyene is a ghost town, and is now incorporated in the City of Dallas. It's on Highway 252, and has a population of 150. It used to be plenty wild."

I thank Miss Mary-Louise Giraud, Tensas Parish Library, St. Joseph, Louisiana, for information about Cole's days in that state.

I checked up as best I could on what he set down in his book by the information that is available today. His locations do not correspond with the locations as they are today. He was writing thirty-eight years later and had, no doubt, only his memory to depend on. Miss Giraud writes: "As to the 'Widow Amos Farm' —no records here as to such a farm, or plantation, and our records in this parish go back to 1843. Fortune Fork, or Creek, is the name of a plantation in Madison Parish, on Walnut Bayou, but as a name of a stream of water it does not appear on any map of Tensas Parish, or Tensas-Concordia Parish. As to the Bass Farm, East Carroll Parish old-timers here say that the family are still in the parish. Lake Providence is the parish seat. You speak also of the William Dickerson Farm, near Floyd, East Carroll Parish. Nothing is known of this family or any plantation by that name. But that does not prove such a man and such a plantation did not exist."

CHAPTER 5

The old bell mentioned in this chapter is now in the entrance to the Carthage High School.

The following clipping also indicates when John Shirley shook the Carthage dust from his heels. It's from the *Carthage Banner*, for June 3, 1886: "Belle Starr, the noted female bandit, is on trial at Fort Smith, Arkansas, charged with a complicity of crimes. She does not give her maiden name but says she was born in Carthage and that her father moved from Carthage to Texas in 1863."

My thanks to Ward L. Schrantz for reviewing this chapter. He is the authority on Belle Starr in her Carthage days. He moves toward a historical statement as cautiously as an Indian on his quarry. Mr. Schrantz is author of *Jasper County, Missouri, in the Civil War*. He lives in Carthage. He says, "Your general picture of John Shirley and Belle fits in with my own. I'm glad you didn't fall into the trap of saying that Mrs. Shirley's given name was Elizabeth, as most writers do. It was the one used by the Fox writers and ever since has been bobbing along on the current of history. Her name appears many times here in Carthage in old county records in relation to property transactions. It was, as you say, Eliza. One more item: it should be remembered there were two battles of Newtonia. This often unhorses writers."

The following deals with the shooting of Bud Shirley and seems to be about as close as one can come to the kernel of truth. It was sent to me by Miss Jessie Stemmons of the Carthage Public Library. She found the item in a scrapbook; seemingly the clipping was from the *Carthage Evening Press* about 1934. The story deals with the man who guided the Union soldiers to what became young Shirley's death. The man was T. C. Wooten of Company C, 15th Missouri Cavalry (Captain Green C. Stotts' company), which was stationed at Cave Springs, Missouri. This is Wooten's story:

"I was present when Bud Shirley was killed at Sarcoxie. He was the brother of Myra Shirley who later became Belle Starr. I had lived in Sarcoxie and knew all about the town, and guided the group of our men who went into town that night to catch some guerrillas said to be sleeping in a house there. We went up by the old mill, and tied our horses there. Then went on foot around to the other side opposite from Cave Springs, then went into town and surrounded the house. The Bushwhackers came out running and, while a great many of us were shooting, we always thought it was Gilbert Schooling who killed Shirley. Schooling took careful aim at Shirley but held his fire until Shirley started to jump a plank fence, then let him have it. Shirley fell dead on the other side."

It is worth noting that the old *Police Gazette* is chiefly responsible for the distortions about Belle. Later writers have put them on their shoulders and carried them cheerily along.

The dates of Cole's comings and goings in Texas are, in main, from his booklet. He forgot to tell of his pleasant hours with the inspiring Belle.

The material about Cole's gun fight is taken from Belle's obituary in the *Fort Smith Weekly Elevator* published a few days after her death. It was written by the editor of the paper, J. W. Weaver, who knew her quite well and who knew the story about Pearl.

William Elliott, who lived on South Eighth Street, Henryetta, Oklahoma, was interviewed April 15, 1937, for the *Indian-Pioneer History*. He was considered an "old-timer." His statement appears in Vol. 23, page 336: "Everybody in our section knew that Pearl was Cole and Belle's child."

When George W. Mayes was interviewed for the *Indian-Pioneer History*, Vol. 71, page 40, he was living at 306 East Thirteenth Street, Oklahoma City. He was eighty-nine years old. He said, "Belle Starr had a daughter by Cole Younger."

From the obituary of Belle Starr in the *Fort Smith Weekly Elevator*, February 1889: "Belle was married in her girlhood to a dashing captain of Quantrill's cutthroat band.... Belle was eighteen when she met and fell in love with Cole Younger and was married to him on horseback." (AUTHOR'S NOTE: This latter statement has been published many times, but it is not correct. There was no horseback ceremony with Cole.)

CHAPTER 6

Jesse's letter mentioning where he and Frank were at the time of the Russellville affair appeared in the *Nashville Banner*, July 10, 1875.

The statement that the men never hid in caves was told to me by Robert F. James, son of Frank James.

Cole's visit to Russellville, Kentucky, is chiefly from the *Kansas City Journal* for April 6, 1882, from Edwin Finch's book, *Kentucky All Over*, and from material supplied me by letter from John W. Muir of Bardstown, Kentucky.

The story of Cole and George Shepherd and their fitful night of rest was told to me by Cole's nephew Harry Younger Hall, whose address has already been given. He said the incident happened in 1872.

The Kansas City fairground robbery is based on a rather complete account in the *Kansas City Journal* for April 6, 1882. Also on an interview with W. T. Singleton, an eyewitness, quoted in the *Kansas City Star*.

CHAPTER 7

As to the Sainte Genevieve affair, I have followed, in main, the account in the *St. Joseph Herald* for April 4, 1882. I have also a letter from Harry J. Petresquin, the attorney for the bank, giving me some additional information. Among other things, he says: "We still have, in our museum, the old safe that gave up some money that day."

CHAPTER 8

The story of Cole as an "eye doctor" was told to me by Otto Ernest Rayburn who is an authority on the Ozarks and is publisher of *Rayburn's Ozark Guide*, Eureka Springs, Arkansas. He said that he was a schoolteacher from 1936 to 1940 in Caddo Gap and heard the story from the old-timers.

From the *Dallas News* for June 7, 1886: "When Belle was eighteen years of age she fell in love with a dashing guerrilla whose name, she said, was not necessary for her to give."

From the *Fort Smith Elevator*, Fort Smith, Arkansas, for May 30, 1886: In an interview Belle said that the first man she ever fell in love with and the first man she married was a noted guerrilla.

Burton Rascoe in his book *Belle Starr*, page 116, says: "At no time did Belle, or anyone else, refer to her daughter as Pearl Reed, but always as Pearl Younger."

From the *Fort Smith Weekly Elevator*, February 10, 1889: "When Belle was eighteen she fell in love with Cole Younger, who was one of the most daring of the guerrillas."

An interview with Mrs. Fannie Blythe Marks, 427 North Thompson Street, Vinita, Oklahoma, was given September 9, 1937, and appears in the *Indian-Pioneer History*, Vol. 3, page 83, on file in the Oklahoma Historical Society, Oklahoma City. "My husband was a deputy United States marshal. Belle Starr once told my husband that she was the wife of Cole Younger."

As to the identification of the body: This from McKinney, Texas, to the *Galveston Daily News*, Sunday, August 9, 1874: "Last night the remains of Jim Reed, the mail robber, arrived here from Paris, Texas, near which place he had been apprehended and shot; and were buried today, after having been fully identified by those who knew him. He was a noted but desperate character, and the citizens are truly glad at the riddance."

Travis Carrol Ely, Speer, Oklahoma, in an interview given March 19, 1938, quoted in the *Indian-Pioneer History*, Vol. 91, page 109: "I was a deputy United States marshal and knew Belle Starr. She ran with Cole Younger a good deal."

To Miss Mildred Stevenson, of the Rosenberg Library, Galveston, Texas: Thanks for digging up for me, in the newspaper quoted, the true story of Reed's death and burial.

"She has one daughter named Pearl Younger, a beautiful girl, possessing her mother's fire and her father's reckless criminality." From the *Fort Smith Weekly Elevator*, in its obituary account. The paper did not seem to recognize it was not paying Pearl much of a compliment when it said she had "her father's reckless criminality."

Harry C. Hoffman, whose address appears in the first chapter, was for many years a close friend of Cole. When Cole believed he was dying, he sent for Hoffman, who arrived at Cole's house on Sunday. Cole died the following Tuesday. Mr. Hoffman wrote me: "Cole often told me that Belle Starr was his 'best girl friend.' But he never mentioned Pearl."

NOTE: This John Fisher is not to be confused with the famous John King Fisher who, at one time, was deputy sheriff of Uvalde County, Texas, and who was killed at the same time as Ben Thompson was, in San Antonio. Little is known about our marrying Fisher, probably no great loss.

CHAPTER 9

A letter to the author from Mrs. John F. Rafferty, 856 West Vernon Avenue, Los Angeles: "My husband is the son of the engineer who was killed. He heard the story from his mother. He says you should bring out that his father could have saved his life if he had deserted his engine and jumped. He was a hero, but is not usually given credit for sticking to his post at the cost of his life."

The statement about Jesse carting the detective's body across the river so that Jesse wouldn't be suspected is from Cole's book itself.

The story of the Otterville holdup was told to me personally by Asbury Good-Knight. This was in Sedalia, Missouri, in 1948, when Mr. Good-Knight was eighty-nine. He had been walking, as a lad, along the railroad track when the James-Youngers seized him, and made him wave a red lantern which, along with the burning ties, was used to stop the train. The date: July 7, 1876.

Memo on Augustus C. Appler, who made Cole so much trouble: Appler was an itinerant newspaperman, born in Carroll County, Maryland, January 1, 1828. He was publisher, for a time, of the *Carroll County Democrat*. He sold the paper and moved to St. Louis, where he got a job as foreman of the *Missouri Republican*. In 1858 he became editor and publisher of the *Hannibal Daily Democrat*. He lost the property. After a time he moved to Osceola, Missouri, where he purchased the *Osceola Weekly Democrat*, which he published from 1872 to 1876. It was during this time that he wrote the Younger book. He returned to St. Louis where he wrote articles for the *St. Louis Times*. In St. Louis he made his home with his daughter, Mrs. H. B. Essington. He died April 18, 1917, at the age of eighty-five, and was buried in Valhalla Cemetery, St. Louis. (This information is from his granddaughter, Mrs. George W. Davies, Osceola, Missouri.)

From Floyd C. Shoemaker, secretary, the State Historical Society of Missouri: "I note that you say you can't get straightened out the name of the Osceola paper that Appler worked on. That's understandable. From July 1871 through June 1873 the name of the paper was the *Osceola Weekly Democrat*. From July 1873 through 1876 the title was the *Osceola Democrat*. Does that untangle it?"

Another book of this period was *The Border Outlaws. An Authentic and Thrilling History of the Most Notorious Bandits of Ancient and Modern Times, the Younger Brothers, Jesse and Frank James, and Their Comrades in Crime* by James William Buel. (They liked long titles then.) It was published in St. Louis in 1881. It is unreliable. *Personal Note:* I was shocked when I found that Buel had once been a reporter on my old paper, the *Kansas City Star*. In my day, if we'd turned in inventions like those in his book we wouldn't have lasted the week out. He does not use the fifteen Union prisoners' story, nor the plank fence story; these were the exclusive property of Appler.

Another book about the Youngers purporting to be reliable was *Adventures and Exploits of the Younger Brothers, Missouri's Most Daring Outlaws and Companions of the James Boys* by Henry Dale. (Another nice mouth-filling title.) The book was published in June 1890. Truth creeps in here.

CHAPTER 10

The physical description of Charlie Pitts is from *The Review*, Mankato, Minnesota, September 26, 1876. It was written by J. A. Clarke, a reporter, who viewed the body.

Charlie Pitts's real name was Sam Wells and Bill Chadwell's real name was William Stiles. The two have gone down in history under their "professional" names. Charlie Pitts had been born and brought up in Independence a few miles from Kansas City where the great outlaws came from.

The information about Cole and Charlie Pitts tossing coins is from the Potter book. The incident was told to him by Cole himself.

My thanks to Robert Steele Withers, Liberty, Missouri, for the information about Clell Miller. Mr. Withers has the old blacksmith's journal. I examined it. One item reads: "This day I made for Ryland Shackleford a frizzen for his flint lock gun." I can't find anyone who knows what a frizzen is.

Close readers may check me up on the dun horse statement. In *Jesse James Was My Neighbor* I said that Jesse was on the horse. I now wish to retract that and to say it was Frank. Since making the former statement I have come upon new information. Even now I am not at liberty to divulge its sources. But it is, I feel, correct, and so I wish to make the change.

This chapter was read for me by Warden Douglas C. Rigg. His comment: "Anent the street fighting. A rifle is superior to a pistol, generally; so against rifles, the pistol-packing Missourians

were against superior fire. Shotguns would be deadly only at
short range."

CHAPTER 11

The story of the sad end of Charlie Pitts is to be found in Dr.
Hoyt's book *A Frontier Doctor*, as told by himself. Also my
thanks to Paul Light, columnist for the *St. Paul Pioneer Press* for
inspiring his readers to come up with sidelights on the story.

The story of Bill Chadwell and his unhappy end came from
Herman Roe of Northfield, who got it from Dr. Wheeler himself when Mr. Roe went to Grand Forks to attend a press
convention.

CHAPTER 12

In the *Kansas City Post*, March 21, 1915 (a year before he
died), Cole gave an interview in which he said that he had been
wounded eleven times at Northfield.

Much of the information in this chapter is from *The Review*,
Mankato, Minnesota, dated September 26, 1876. The dispatch
is headed "Madelia, Sep, 21, 5:30 P.M." and would seem to have
been the first on-the-spot reporting of the capture of the men.
The paper itself, a weekly, was not published until September 26,
as shown above. The dispatch is signed by J. A. Clarke, the
reporter who interviewed the bandits.

The story of the man hunt has been put together from
material in the *St. Paul Pioneer Press*, the *Faribault Republican*,
and *The Review*, a weekly published in Mankato.

Cole in his book tells how Jesse James wanted to kill Jim.

G. W. Walrath lived at Morristown, Minnesota, fifteen miles
from Northfield. He was a member of the party that helped to
capture Bob Younger. Mr. Walrath said that Bob Younger told
him personally that Jesse James wanted to kill Jim Younger.

Later, Mr. Walrath was foreman of the grand jury that indicted the Youngers.

The story of the whistle is from *The Review*, September 26.

The story of the women weeping in the courtroom was told by Foreman Walrath in an interview in the *Kansas City Star*, for later he moved to Missouri and often talked of the pursuit and capture.

The reports in the *Pioneer Press* and *The Review* are, in main, the same. It would seem that *The Review* was using some of the *Pioneer Press* material.

A note as to the handing out of the reward money: The governor of Minnesota offered, in the name of the state, a reward of $4,000. The state delayed payment and the politicians got their fingers into the pie. The people who had helped capture the outlaws demanded their money. The politicians said that certain points had to be settled first. The captors had to sue in the courts to get their money. Finally some money was dribbled down to the captors who had been, after all, pretty brave men. The posse that actually laid hands on Cole and his brothers got $240 each.

Thirty-nine others who had taken part, one way or another, got $56.25 each.

Eight each got $15.

Axel Oscar Sorbel, the boy who helped, got $56.25.

When the men came back from the great man hunt they were lauded in the streets and called "our heroes." Well, it took the heroes just a year and a half to get their money—so much for heroism, when the time comes to pay out the money.

CHAPTER 13

The story of Jesse James and Belle in the gambling hall is from information given me by Frank James's son, Robert F. James, Excelsior Springs, Missouri.

Belle's reference to her son's intelligence is from her letter dated August 19, 1876, written from Dallas.

My thanks to the Cecil Atchison Collection, Fort Smith, Arkansas, for making photographs for me of the document containing Pearl Younger's name. The original petition is falling apart and has to be handled with care.

My thanks to Ross V. Randolph, warden of the Illinois State Penitentiary, Menard Branch, for digging up the facts about Blue Duck's penal troubles.

I asked the one and only Joe Galbreath, robust ranchman of Talala, Oklahoma, to see what he could find out about Blue Duck, firsthand. His letter: "Like I'm always doin' for you, I work hard & get nothing for it, only a copy of your book which is about like workin' on the section at a dollar a day and furnishing your own handcar. I went to see Mrs. Molly Daniels McIntosh, a full-blood, on the Indian Rolls as Number 25240. I've known her for years, but had to get one of her five daughters to interpret for me, as I don't talk Indian good, like I do English. Molly knew Blue Duck when she was a young girl. She said he was six feet tall, weighed about 180, wore his hair coiled up in his hat. His Indian name was *Sha-con-gah Kaw-wan-nu,* which in English means Blue Duck. There was a large family of *Sha-con-gahs.* One time a white woman and an Indian girl stopped at Molly's grandmother's for a meal. The Indian girl was Jennie Duck, Blue's sister. The white woman couldn't talk Indian. Her name was Belle Starr. She said that Belle was nice-mannered and pleasant to have to a meal. Molly said that she shook a tree limb over the table to keep the flies off. When your book is printed, send me a copy and someday I will glance through some of it."

The hymnbook story appears in the *Dallas News,* January 9, 1927, signed by Vivian Richardson.

The story of Officer Marks's tussle with Belle is told in the *Indian-Pioneer History,* Vol. 16, page 89.

Also the story was told to me in person by Elias Rector, 1455 North 39th Street, Fort Smith. When I talked to him he was past ninety and was one of the last surviving marshals of Judge Parker's fabulous court. His story, in main, was the same as the one I have used, except he said that Belle had only one pistol nestled in her bosom.

In *Hell on the Border* S. W. Harman says he copied Belle's letter from the original in Fort Smith. No one has ever seen the letter; he is the only person to say it ever existed. I don't believe that Belle would place-date a letter "Pandemonium." In fact, I don't think she could spell it, even if she knew what it meant. And why should not the date be put in? And why should she sign the letter "Belle Starr" instead of Mother? Belle could not write so grammatically as the letter has her doing. But of course the letter might have been edited; in fact, it shows this all the way through; some places the word is *wont;* other places *won't.* I have puzzled and puzzled over the letter and have come to the conclusion that it was invented by Harman.

According to the Canadian County, Cherokee Census, for 1890, Mr. and Mrs. Barnes were full-blooded Cherokees. The wife's first name was Wynona.

Frog Hoyt's real name was Milo A. Hoyt. He was a full-blooded Choctaw who ran the ferry and, at the time of the killing of Belle Starr, was considered the wealthiest man in the community. He died in Pauls Valley, Oklahoma, in 1927. There is a town named for him.

In describing the murder of Belle Starr on the lonely road I have followed, in main, the material discovered by Frederick S. Barde, who got together the "Barde Collection" and who, for twenty years, ran down every item he could about Belle Starr. His material—unpublished—is now in the Oklahoma Historical Society, where I examined it. Mr. Barde died in Guthrie in 1916. His daughter, Miss Letha Barde, Broadmoor Hotel, Oklahoma City, told me her father gathered his information about Belle and Oklahoma history by traveling through Oklahoma by spring wagon or on horseback, interviewing old settlers, and talking to the Indians. Sometimes he sat on a stump and made notes as the people talked.

For the details of the actual burial I have followed an eye-

witness account that appeared in the *Tahlequah Telephone*,
March 1, 1889. This account gives the fascinating details of the
armed pallbearers and the cornbread. Tahlequah was the capital
of the Cherokee Nation and the *Telephone* was published there.

On her way home, that fateful day, Belle also stopped at the
home of a man named Rowe. (Some writers set it down as
Rose.)

I found the following item in an old scrapbook owned by
Martin E. Ismert, 51 West 53rd Street Terrace, Kansas City,
Missouri. He is an authority on the outlaws of the Middle Border,
and here and now I want to thank him for the leg up he gave me.
The item does not reveal the name of the paper. The item:

"Fort Smith, Ark. Feb 4, 1889. Jim Starr, a United States
witness, today received a telegram from Eufaula, I. T., that Belle
Starr had been killed there last night. Belle was the wife of Cole
Younger." What must Jim have thought when the telegram to
him proclaimed his Belle as the wife of another? (PERSONAL
OPINION: I think the telegram was sent by Pearl.—The Author.)

The statement that Jim July-Starr pointed his rifle at Watson
and arrested him is from an interview with W. S. Hall who was
present. He was the postmaster at Whitefield, with the post office
in his store, and it was from him that Belle got her mail. Mr.
Hall says that Watson was calmly banking up Belle's grave when
Jim "pulled down" on him. The interview appeared in the *Tulsa
World*, April 13, 1930, while Mr. Hall was still living. He is
also the authority for the statement about the theft of the pistol.

The place where the bloody Watson lived was in the section
that Barron G. Collier bought in 1922—a million acres. He was
a rich New York advertising man. A county is now named after
him; Everglades is its seat.

CHAPTER 14

The prison entry for Jim Younger is as follows: Prison number
—700; age—28 years; height—5 feet 9 inches; occupation—

farmer; native—Missouri State. For Bob Younger it reads: Prison number—701; age—22 years; height—5 feet 6 inches; native—Missouri State; occupation—farmer.

Professor Morris's plumbing of Cole's psychology took place May 5, 1890. His report, in manuscript form, is in the Minnesota Historical Society, where I read it. The professor himself lived at 620 West Fifth Street, Winona, Minnesota.

The story of the reporter quizzing Cole on the death of Jesse James is from the *Kansas City Times*, April 4, 1882. A correspondent for the paper went to the prison to see Cole.

The description of Cole in the library is from the *Cincinnati Enquirer*, January 29, 1899.

The interview with Cole, when Belle's death was announced, is from the *Stillwater Daily Gazette*, February 6, 1889. The St. Paul and Minneapolis papers also carried accounts of Belle's death and Cole's comments, but the one from the *Gazette* is more detailed.

Much of the material about Bronaugh's amazing struggle to get Cole out of prison is from Bronaugh's book, *The Youngers' Fight for Freedom*. The book was published in 1906 by himself, printed by the E. W. Stephens Publishing Company, Columbia, Missouri. The book is now a collector's prayer.

The story of Cole's release is from the *Kansas City Star*, July 11, 1901. The paper sent a reporter there to cover the story; he deals with the event at some length. I have used only a fragment of his detailed story.

Some of the new wonders that Cole saw that day are reported in the *St. Louis Republic*, July 14, 1901. The paper had a reporter there.

My thanks to Miss Gertrude Glennon, Stillwater, Minnesota, whose father Jack Glennon was deputy warden when Cole was in prison. She passed along to me stories that her father had told her about the Youngers.

And my thanks to Warden Douglas C. Rigg of the Minnesota State Prison, at Stillwater. I stayed with him two days, my eyes popping the whole time. And my thanks to R. F. Farnham, records officer, who brought out enough old papers, records, and documents to fill a naphtha launch.

CHAPTER 15

The Records Office at the state prison in Minnesota has about a dozen of Cole's monthly reports to the warden.

An example of how bumbling later outlaws were, the career of the Jennings brothers can be cited. They "rode" in 1897. Their criminal career lasted three and a half months and their entire "take" was $300. It must have made Cole, in Minnesota, smile.

The Dalton boys were small fry. In October 1892 six of the Dalton Gang rode into Coffeyville, Kansas, bent on robbing two banks at the same time. They would show the James-Youngers up as amateurs. Out came the trusty grain sack, just as the James-Youngers used it. When the matter was over, four of them lay on the streets, dead as ducks; the fifth, Emmett Dalton, had as many holes in him as a colander. The sixth one, George Padgett, got away. All of the money was recovered except twenty dollars. Again Cole must have smiled.

The story of the wonderful coal-oil burner was told by Will R. Robison of Muskogee in an interview given February 24, 1937. It appears in *Indian-Pioneer History*, Vol. 8, Oklahoma Historical Society.

I was stumped as to what a "Coliseum" was, so I appealed to Elmer L. Pigg, who is an almanac of outlaw information. He says: "This term was often used by carnivals in this section of the Midwest. It was a sideshow. Here Cole had on exhibition guns, saddles, and spurs as used by outlaws. The people would come in and Cole would explain the use of the different articles. But they came more to see Cole, close up, than the exhibits."

The story of Cole and the ruffians was told to me by Harry C. Hoffman, who said that Cole and Frank James, on account of this, left the show. He said that the show management threatened to sue and that Cole and Frank employed Judge John Phillips to defend them. The show management decided that the matter would be spread by the newspapers, and so dropped the threatened suit.

Robertus Love has the same story in *The Rise and Fall of Jesse James*, but says it happened in northern Missouri; also says this was why Cole and Frank quit the show.

Robertus Love says that Cole died with seventeen bullets in him. Cole himself gave the number as "more than a dozen."

Cole's later days were described to me by Miss Mary Jo Ragsdale, daughter of Cole's doctor.

I want to thank two men for help, and here's as good a place as any to do so. First is B. J. George, 3 East 65th Terrace, Kansas City 13, Missouri. He is the greatest living authority on Quantrill; in fact, his father rode with Quantrill. B. J.'s patience in going through old files of the *Independence Examiner*, the *Blue Springs Herald*, and the *Oak Grove Banner*, looking for goodies, passeth my understanding. His patience and industry made me feel like a sluggard.

Second. My thanks to Martin E. Ismert, 51 West 53rd Street Terrace, Kansas City 12, Missouri, who has the greatest outlaw collection I ever saw. I spent three evenings with him, popeyed. I want to thank him for the pictures he pulled out of his collection for me; they have never heretofore been published. Fine man.

CHAPTER 16

In the part about the visit to Belle Starr's grave, the sources are shown in the text.

My thanks to the Public Library, Douglas, Arizona, for turning up the facts about Pearl Younger's death and burial. And so the little family of three is buried in three different states: Oklahoma, Missouri, and Arizona.

The exact location of Pearl Younger's grave in Calvary Cemetery, in Douglas, Arizona, is Lot 7, Block 61, Section F.

Chapters 17 and 18 are mostly matters of opinion.

Index

Glennon, Miss Gertrude (she helped me greatly), 232

H

Hall, Harry Younger (Cole's nephew), 183

Hamilton, Claude A., 199

Harman, S. W. (in his life of Belle Starr he rewrote the Richard K. Fox maunderings), 51, 230

Harris, H. Clay, 183

Hays, Upton B., 17, 18, 20

He Hanged Them High (a book about Hanging Judge Isaac C. Parker; recommended), 91

Hell's Corner (a part of Missouri, justly named), 38

Higgins, Mrs. Gertrude, 90

Hoffman, Harry C., 5, 84, 196, 216, 224, 234

How the soldiers lived, 26

Hudspeth, Silas (an outlaw could always get shelter there), 76

I

Ignatius Donnelly, who proved that Francis Bacon wrote Shakespeare, also proves that Cole was unjustly imprisoned, 170

"Ironclad Oath," 44

Ismert, Martin E. (he helped me mightily), 12, 231

J

James, Frank (Cole's friend; Cole did not get along with Jesse), 32, 44, 47, 65, 158, 181

James, Robert F. (Frank's son), 222, 228

Jarrett, Captain (leader of the Bushwhackers), 17

Jayhawker (that's somebody from Kansas), 6, 7, 35, 43, 101

Jefferson Davis (you'll be surprised how he got in here), 31

Jennison, 7

Jesse James (Kearney boy), 33, 44, 61, 64, 66, 67

Jesse James Was My Neighbor (recommended), 226

Jesse threatens to kill Cole's brother, 124

Jim Cummins (a cry-baby among bandits), 182

Jim July gets himself married to Belle Starr, 148, 154

Judge Parker (there is a good book about him), 150

K

Can't find anything for this.

L

Lane, Senator Jim (a strange character, sometimes called "Old Jim Lane"), 28, 34, 58

Lawrence, Amos A. (Lawrence, Kansas, gets its name from him), 31

Lee, General Robert E. (he gets in because of his beard), 4, 41

Lone Jack (a Southern Missouri town, also a battle), 20, 21, 23, 164, 165, 169

Reed, Jim (Belle Starr married
him on horseback, with a bunch
of outlaws as bridesmaids), 86,
88, 89, 90, 148

Reed, William M. (Jim Reed's
cousin tells firsthand story), 89,
92

Richey, Matthew H., 51, 53

Russellville, Kentucky (Cole makes
a professional call on the bank),
68, 75

S

Sainte Genevieve, Missouri (The
Boys called there), 78

Schrantz, Ward L., historian, 220

Shakespeare (about the last place
you'd expect to find him), 105

Shaner, Dolph, 82

Shelby, General Jo (celebrated
Missouri general), 17, 18

Shepherd, George R. (one of
Jesse's boys), 15, 32, 42, 75,
222

Shirley, John (Belle Starr's
father), 39, 49, 56, 57, 58, 59

Shoemaker, Floyd C., noted historian, 225

Sitting Bull (gets in by a hair), 98

Six Mile Church, 10

Starr, Sam (one of Belle's husbands), 143

Starr, Tom (cruelest man in the
Indian Territory and Belle's
father-in-law), 138

Starr, Belle (she had a Big Romance with Cole), 5, 38, 49,
61, 67, 133; meets Jesse James,

134; her marriage record, 139,
198

Stemmons, Miss Jessie, 220

Stevenson, Miss Mildred, 223

Stomp dance (what happened at
it), 147

Stillwater Prison reaches out for
Cole, 158

Suse (she becomes a character in
this story), 23, 24, 25

T

"Take to the brush" (everybody
knew what that meant), 8

Tombstones (Cole gets a job selling them), 177

Todd, George (one of the bad
ones), 27, 42

Truman, Harry S (has farm near
Cole's), 4

Twyman, Mrs. T. W. (Cole's
aunt), 9

U

Uncle Cole (anecdote told about
him by his nephew), 187

V

Virgin material is in this book.

W

Walley, Irvin (Cole's enemy), 8

Watt Grayson, Indian (Belle
robbed him), 91

La End